The
Hidden
Glory *of*
India

Readers interested in the subject matter of this book are invited to correspond with the publisher at one of the following addresses:

The Bhaktivedanta Book Trust
P. O. Box 34074
Los Angeles, CA 90034, USA
Phone: +1-800-927-4152
Fax: +1-310-837-1056
E-mail: bbt.usa@krishna.com

The Bhaktivedanta Book Trust
Korsnäs Gård
14792 Grödinge, Sweden
Phone: +46-8-53029800
Fax: +46-8-53025062
E-mail: bbt.se@krishna.com

The Bhaktivedanta Book Trust
P. O. Box 380
Riverstone, NSW 2765, Australia
Phone: +61-2-96276306
Fax: +61-2-96276052
E-mail: bbt.au@krishna.com

The Bhaktivedanta Book Trust
Hare Krishna Land
Juhu, Mumbai 400049, India
Phone: +91-22-26202921
Fax: +91-22-26200357
E-mail: bbt.in@krishna.com

www.krishna.com

*To Shrila Prabhupada,
who brought
the hidden glory of India
to Western shores.*

*And to Vrinda,
who brought Pratima
to those same shores.*

ISBN 0-89213-351-1

Printed in China

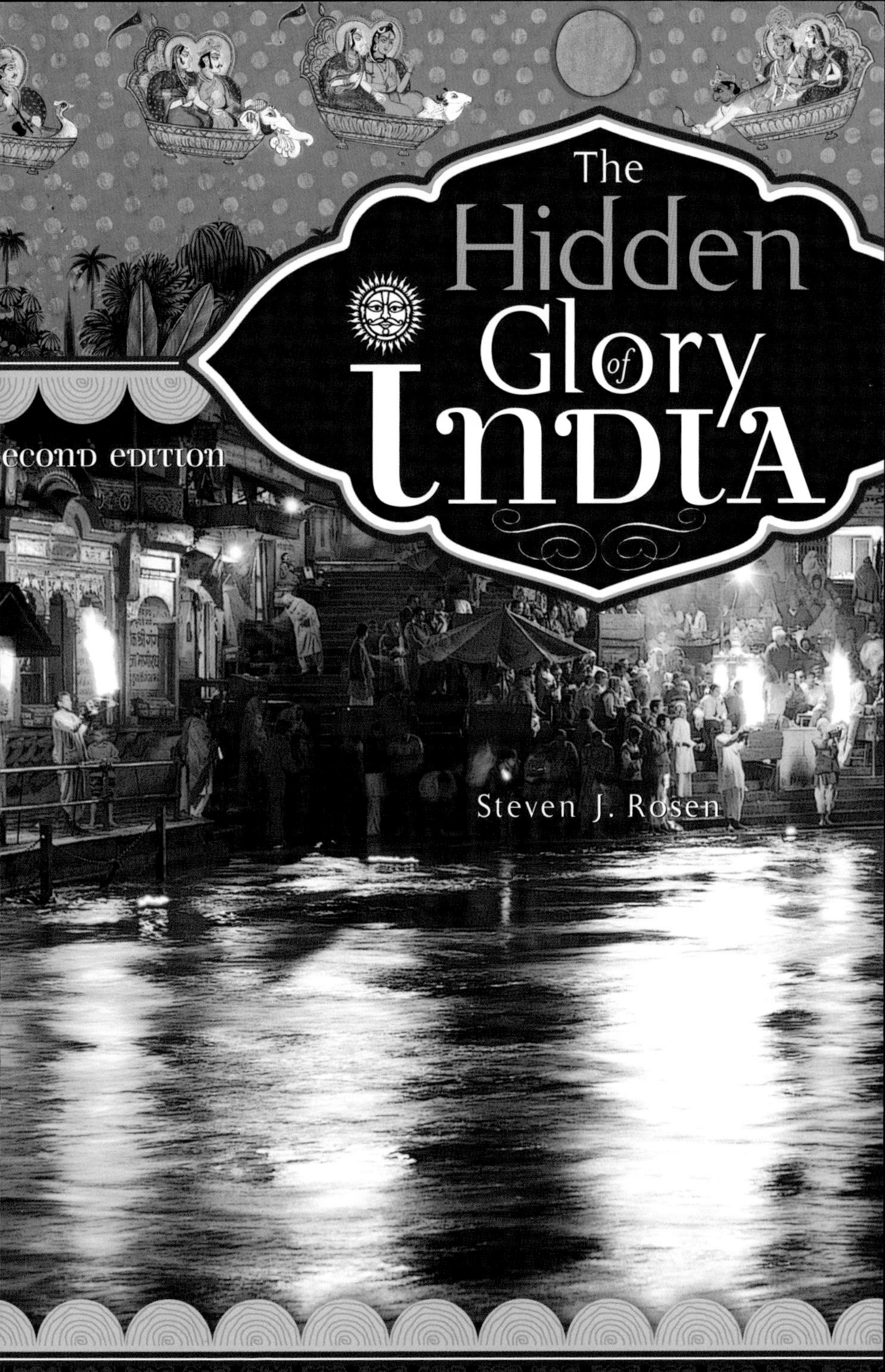

The
Hidden
Glory of
India

Second Edition

Steven J. Rosen

THE BHAKTIVEDANTA BOOK TRUST

contents

6   INTRODUCTION
8   SPIRITUAL INDIA
10   "HINDUISM"

SACRED TEXTS: 1

14   The Vedic Literature
16   Shrimad Bhagavatam
18   The Bhagavatam:
      Its Contents
20   The Mahabharata
22   The Bhagavad-gita
24   Gita Commentaries
26   Ramayana
28   Rama Retellings

VAISHNAVA ROOTS: 2

32   Early Vaishnavism:
      Southern Roots
34   Early Vaishnavism:
      Northern Roots
36   Buddha and Shankara
38   Acharyas

THE GODHEAD: 3

42   Three Aspects of God
44   Three Aspects:
      An Analogy
46   Shri Krishna
48   Expansions of Krishna
50   Avatars of Vishnu
52   Nrisimha Avatar
54   The Original Goddess
56   Radha
58   The Gopis
60   Tulasi Devi

THE DEMIGODS: 4

64   Demigods
66   Shiva
68   Durga
70   Maya
72   Ganesh
74   Brahma
76   Sarasvati
78   Hanuman

TIME AND SPACE: 5

82   The Four Ages
84   Time
86   Vedic Cosmology
88   The Spiritual Sky
90   Karma and Reincarnation

THE HIDDEN INCARNATION: 6

94 Shri Chaitanya:
     An Introduction
96 Shri Chaitanya: His Life
98 Shri Chaitanya:
     His Teachings
100 The Six Goswamis
102 Bhakti:
     Devotional Love

SACRED PLACES: 7

106 Temples
108 Sacred Architecture
110 Vrindavan
112 Navadvip
114 Mayapur
116 The Ganges
118 Jagannath Puri
120 The Festival of the Chariots
122 Travel Information

THE ARTS: 8

126 Fine Arts
128 Poetry
130 Drama
132 Dance
134 Music

PRACTITIONERS: 9

138 What Is a Devotee?
140 The Guru Principle
142 Shrila Prabhupada
144 Sadhus
146 Women
148 Jesus in India?

PRACTICES AND TEACHINGS: 10

152 Varnashrama
154 Yoga
156 The Yoga System:
     The Eight Steps of
     Ashtanga-Yoga
158 Meditation
160 Mandalas and Yantras
162 Idols and Deities
164 Deity Worship
166 Language
168 Dress
170 Sacred Cow
172 Vegetarianism
174 Festivals
176 The Modes of Nature
178 Ayurveda
180 Vedic Astrology
182 The Gayatri Mantra
184 Sound
186 Chanting
188 The Maha-mantra

190 AFTERWORD
192 CREDITS

Introduction

In the 1950s, an Austrian scholar named Walther Eidlitz published a book called Unknown India. He writes of his quest for truth and of his subsequent relationship with Shri Maharaj—his guru, whom he met in the Himalayas in the 1930s. The story is familiar: a Western seeker finds an Indian teacher and decides to adopt a traditional form of Eastern spirituality.

But the story continues. As the years pass, Eidlitz finds himself in an India beset by World War II and is placed in a prison camp for nearly six years. During his internment he meets Sadananda, a German gentleman in Indian dress, who is also a prisoner. They forge a friendship, and Sadananda introduces Eidlitz to Vaishnavism ("the worship of Vishnu, or Krishna"). Sadananda had been initiated into this esoteric tradition by Shrila Bhaktisiddhanta Sarasvati Thakur, a saint and scholar from Bengal, and was anxious to share his knowledge with others, specifically with Eidlitz. Eidlitz comes to call Sadananda's zealousness "aggressive grace."

Impressed by Sadananda's knowledge and wisdom, Eidlitz feels that Sadananda has augmented the knowledge received from Shri Maharaj, and consequently accepts Sadananda as his new guru. Thus, "the unknown India" that Eidlitz writes about is not the exotic land itself, nor is it the teachings commonly associated with Hinduism. Rather, Eidlitz comes to see Vaishnavism as the hidden glory of India.

Still, one wonders why Vaishnavism would be considered "hidden." The 1996 Britannica Book of the Year asserts that Vaishnavas make up 70% of the 800 million Hindu constituency (25% are Shaivites, worshipers of Shiva; 2% are neo-Hindus or reform Hindus of various leanings; and the balance is made up of adherents to other Indic faiths). Thus, Vaishnavism constitutes the majority of the Hindu world. Nonetheless, the West is unfamiliar not only with the term "Vaishnavism" but with the tradition it denotes. The obscurity of Vaishnavism is in part due to the 1893 World Parliament of Religions Conference in Chicago, which hosted Swami

Shrila Bhaktisiddhanta Saraswati Thakur, guru of Sadananda.

Vivekananda of the Ramakrishna Mission as India's representative of Hinduism. At that conference, Vivekananda popularized for the West a Hinduism that embraced a plethora of gods and ultimately Advaita Vedanta (an impersonalist view of reality). Had a Vaishnava been invited to that consequential gathering of religious representatives, we in the West might now have a very different perspective on Hinduism.

Vaishnavism, in sharp contrast to the "Hinduism" of Vivekananda, is not only monotheistic but highly personalistic in its view of God— Krishna may have expansions and *avatars* (incarnations), but He is seen as the one Supreme Lord, the Father of all that lives and the Creator of the cosmos.

In other words, while Vaishnavism may not be the most well-known form of Hinduism, it is India's richest and most significant religious tradition. Unlike many books that explore India or Eastern spirituality, this work will focus squarely on the Vaishnava tradition, including its most contemporary and far-reaching manifestation—the International Society for Krishna Consciousness (ISKCON), founded in 1966 by His Divine Grace A. C. Bhaktivedanta Swami Prabhupada (referred to popularly as Shrila Prabhupada). Incidentally, Shrila Prabhupada was also initiated by Sadananda's guru, Shrila Bhaktisiddhanta Sarasvati Thakur.

Readers of this work may be familiar with the images of Krishna, Shiva, Ganesh, Brahma, and so on, but now these images will take on a new significance; they will be described in terms of their Vaishnava origin.

Vaishnavism is understood by its practitioners as a universal, non-sectarian theistic tradition. Originally the Vaishnava tradition is called Sanatan Dharma, "the eternal religion," or "the eternal function of the soul." Vaishnavas see it as universal truth, applicable to East and West

While Vaishnavism may not be the most well-known form of Hinduism, it is India's richest and most significant religious tradition.

alike. Krishna, for example, is viewed not as an "Indian" god but as the same God who is worshiped in the Judeo-Christian tradition. Brahma, Shiva, Ganesh, and the other divinities are regarded as highly elevated beings, like angels. It is this all-encompassing Vaishnava spirituality that the present work is meant to convey. Specifically, the focus is on Gaudiya Vaishnavism—the Vaishnava religion propounded by Shri Chaitanya Mahaprabhu (1486–1533), who is revered as an incarnation of Krishna.

Shri Chaitanya Mahaprabhu

SPIRITUAL
INDIA

"Twenty-five centuries ago, at least, it [India] was famous. When Babylon was struggling with Nineveh for supremacy, when Tyre was planting her colonies, when Athens was growing in strength, before Rome had become known, or Greece had contended with Persia, or Cyrus had added luster to the Persian monarchy, or Nebuchadnezzar had captured Jerusalem...she had already **risen** to greatness, if not **glory**." —*M. A. Sherring (1868)*

Spirituality informs all aspects of Indian culture. It permeates family and social life, as well as many major political movements. To the average person living in India, religion is an expression of universal truth, a profound, complex outgrowth of the soul. Indian religion is so all-encompassing that it engages practitioners differently from the Western religious traditions. According to Peter Occhiogrosso, best-selling author and scholar of comparative religion:

In any study of the religions of the world, India deserves special treatment. According to a recent Gallup survey, no country has a higher percentage of respondents who believe that religion is "very important" in their lives. (The United States ranks second.) Of India's approximately 850 million residents [now 1 billion], 680 million [now 800 million plus], over 80 percent, are Hindus. Historians agree that the earliest known civilizations that left written records flourished at about the same time in Mesopotamia and the Indus Valley in northern India. But since we have no record of a mystical religion practiced in Sumer, as we do for the Indus region, the oldest recorded mystical teachings in the world belong to India.[1]

India's timeless spiritual teachings have an allure that has beckoned millions: from seekers trekking high in the snowy Himalayas to austere mendicants meditating on the serene banks of the Ganges.

Notes

1. Peter Occhiogrosso. 1994. *The Joy of Sects: A Spirited Guide to the World's Religious Traditions*, 1. New York: Doubleday.

Zarathustra, emphasized the battle between good and evil. Today there are about 85,000 Parsis in India.

Islamic leaders invaded India in the 12th century. With intermittent success over many centuries, today Muslims constitute 11% of the Indian population. This makes Islam the largest minority religion in the country.

Religion in India

The vast majority of people in India are Hindus (a misnomer, as described on the next page). Hinduism itself is called "a museum of religions." This refers to the fact that under the general name of Hinduism one finds many distinct traditions: the worship of Vishnu (Vaishnavism), the worship of the Goddess (Shaktism), the worship of Shiva (Shaivism), and many minor cults and regional sects.

These religions were born in India, as were several later traditions: Buddhism, Jainism, and Sikhism (the first two are 2,500 years old, and Sikhism emerged in the 15th century). Buddhism and Jainism are primarily concerned with morals and ethics, particularly with *ahimsa*, or harmlessness to all living beings. Sikhism is an interesting blend of Hindu and Islamic beliefs. India is home to roughly six million Buddhists, three million Jains, and sixteen million Sikhs.

India's "adopted" religions—Zoroastrianism, Islam, Christianity, and Judaism—also have a place in her spiritual landscape. Zoroastrianism, or the Parsi religion, arose in ancient Persia. Its founder,

Although it was once believed that Christianity arrived in India with the Apostle Thomas in 52 C.E., many scholars now feel that the religion actually arrived in the 4th century with a Syrian merchant named Thomas Cana who traveled to Kerala with 400 families and established there the Indian Syrian Orthodox Church. Currently, there are about 18 million Christians in India, most of whom reside in the south. The Jewish population in India is negligible (perhaps 25,000 in all); its presence is visible mainly in Marathi- and Malayalam-speaking areas.

Religious celebration at night on the banks of the Manasi-ganga in Govardhan, Uttar Pradesh.

"Hinduism"

It should be pointed out that the word "Hindu" is not found in any of the classical writings of India. Nor can it be traced to the classical Indian languages, such as Sanskrit or Tamil. In fact, the word "Hinduism" has absolutely no origins within India itself. Still, it persists, and traditions as diverse as Shaivism and Jainism, Shaktism and Vaishnavism, have been described as "Hinduism." This may work as a matter of convenience, but ultimately it is inaccurate.

His Divine Grace A.C. Bhaktivedanta Swami Prabhupada, founder and spiritual preceptor of the present-day Hare Krishna movement, saw the word as a misnomer:

"Sometimes Indians both inside and outside India think that we are preaching the Hindu religion, but actually we are not. One will not find the word 'Hindu' in the Bhagavad-gita. Indeed, there is no such word as 'Hindu' in the entire Vedic literature. This word has been introduced by the Muslims from provinces next to India, such as Afghanistan, Baluchistan, and Persia. There is a river called Sindhu bordering the northwestern provinces of India, and since the Muslims there could not pronounce Sindhu properly, they instead called the river 'Hindu,' and the inhabitants of this tract of land they called 'Hindus.'"[1]

Prabhupada's explanation of the word "Hindu" is not his own construction. Such explanations are well known among scholars of the Indian tradition. In *Seven Systems of Indian Philosophy*, for example, Pandit Rajmani Tigunait writes along similar lines:

"…[T]he current popular usage of the term Hinduism does not correspond to its original meaning. When Alexander the Great invaded the subcontinent around 325 B.C.E., he crossed the river Sindhu and renamed it Indus, which was easier for the Greek tongue to pronounce. Alexander's Macedonian forces subsequently called the land to the east of this river India. Later, the Moslem invaders called the Sindhu River the Hindu River because in their language, Parsee, the Sanskrit sound s converts to h. Thus, for the invaders, Sindhu became Hindu, and the land east of that river became known as Hindustan."[2]

The concept is also articulated by historian C. J. Fuller, who underscores the fact that the word "Hindu" originally meant something geographical, not cultural or religious. In addition, he points out the convenient usage of the term in separating Muslims from other peoples in India:

"*The Persian word 'Hindu' derives from Sindhu, the Sanskrit name of the river Indus (in modern Pakistan). It originally meant a native of India, the land around and beyond the Indus. When 'Hindu' (or 'Hindoo') entered the English language in the seventeenth century, it was similarly used to denote any native of Hindustan (India), but gradually came to mean someone who retained the indigenous religion and had not converted to Islam. 'Hinduism,' as a term for that indigenous religion, became current in English in the early nineteenth century and was coined to label an 'ism' that was itself partly a product of western orientalist thought, which (mis)constructed Hinduism on the model of occidental religions, particularly Christianity. Hinduism, in other words, came to be seen as a single system of doctrines, beliefs, and practices properly equivalent to those that make up Christianity, and 'Hindu' now clearly specified an Indian's religious affiliation.*"[3]

Using the overarching term "Hinduism" for the many religions of India is comparable to ignoring the different religious orientations within each of the Western traditions, arbitrarily merging them under a single banner—"Semitism" (which, like "Hinduism," merely denotes geographical location). Judaism, Christianity, Islam, and others constitute the diverse religious traditions of the Western world. Just as the term Semitism is too broad and reductionistic to represent properly the unique religious manifestations of the great Western traditions, and just as it would be inappropriate to refer to all these traditions as one religion, the term Hinduism falls short.

Thus, "Hinduism" is more problematic than "Hindu," since it implies a unified form of Indian religion that can comfortably fit under one banner. Considering the varieties of religion that currently exist in India, such as Vaishnavism and Shaivism, a single term is hardly appropriate.

Notes

1. A. C. Bhaktivedanta Swami Prabhupada. 1977. 'Krishna Consciousness: Hindu Cult or Divine Culture?' In "The Science of Self-Realization," 105. Los Angeles: The Bhaktivedanta Book Trust.

2. Pandit Rajmani Tigunait, "Seven Systems of Indian Philosophy" (Honesdale, Pennsylvania: The Himalayan International Institute of Yoga, 1983), 4–5. See also A. C. Bhaktivedanta Swami Prabhupada. 1977. 'Spiritual Communism.' In "The Science of Self-Realization," 196, where he too talks about the mispronunciation of the "s" and "h" sound.

3. C. J. Fuller. 1992. "The Camphor Flame: Popular Hinduism and Society in India," 10. Princeton University Press.

"A special function of the sacred scriptures is their power to inspire. Reading religious books is an extremely efficacious discipline, for while it educates us, it also rouses our spiritual fervor. Scriptures ignite the fires of our devotion, give us the courage to step up our efforts, even make us feel closer to the Divine then and there. Reading of the exploits of Krishna can be so spiritually delectable one feels a hair's-breadth away from liberation. Pondering an Upanishad passage deeply, one senses that Brahman realization is extremely close at hand. Sacred literature acts as a fuel to keep our spiritual journey at a steady clip."

—Barbara Powell
University of Chicago Divinity School

SACRED TEXTS 1

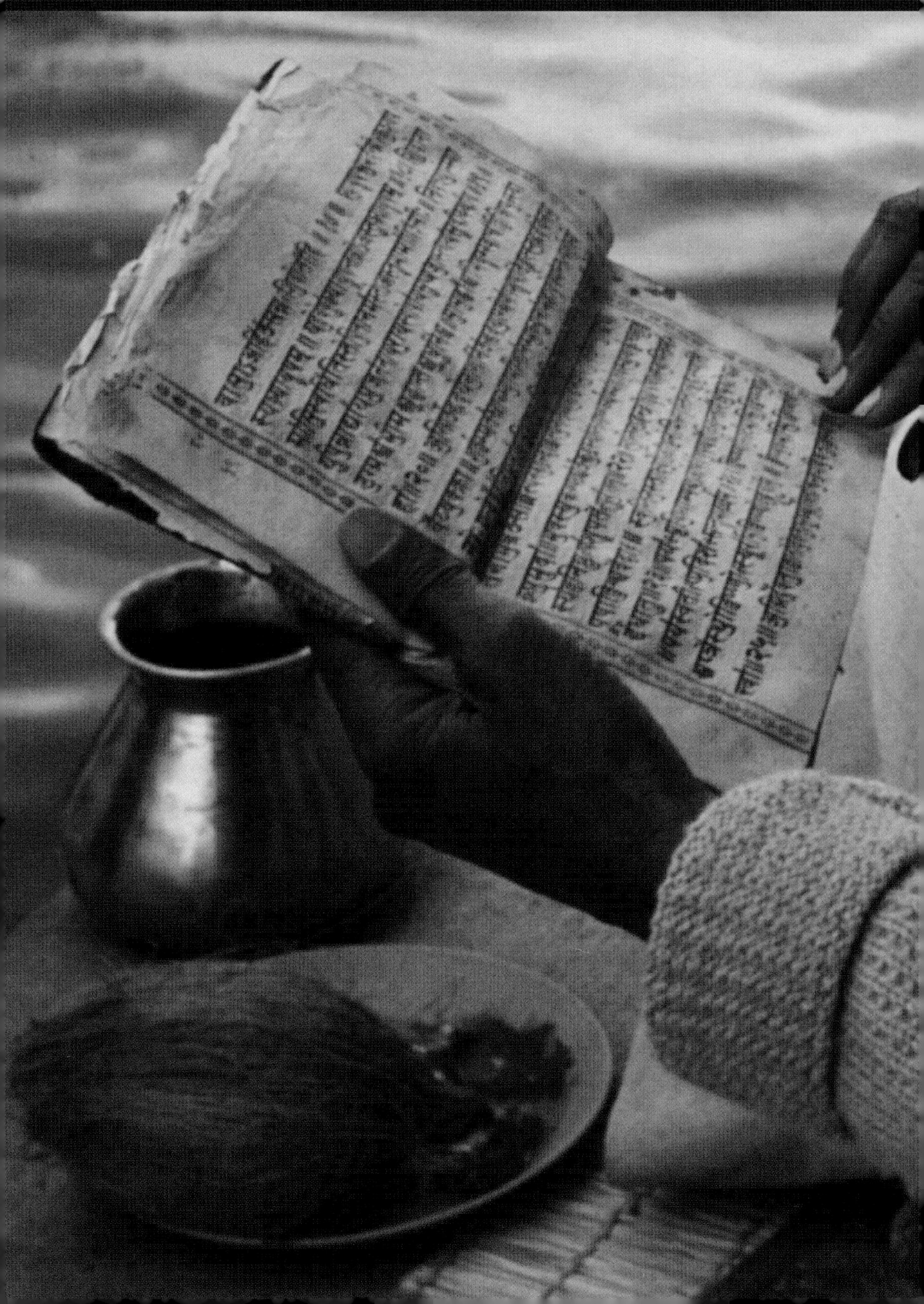

THE VEDIC LITERATURE

In the Indian tradition, the esoteric wisdom of the universe is called Veda. This word can be traced to the Sanskrit root *vid*, which means "to know" or "knowledge." It is related to the words "wit" and "wisdom" from the German; "idea" (originally *widea*) from the Greek; and "video" from the Latin. (One who knows, sees the truth; hence: video.) The holy books of India, containing the essence of Vedic knowledge, are called the Vedas.

According to Vaishnava tradition, the Vedas emanate from the Lord Himself. Vedic knowledge is carefully passed down, from master to disciple; this is called *parampara*, or disciplic succession. The lineages in which the Vedic message is transmitted are called *sampradayas*. In this way, the Vedic prophets sought to maintain the integrity of their oral tradition. The idea is that the Vedas, when properly received in disciplic succession, are devoid of imperfection and interpolation, qualities invariably associated with secular literature.

The Vedic knowledge was given by the Supreme Lord to creator-god Brahma, who in turn gave it to Narada, one of his sons. Narada gave this knowledge to the sage Vyasa, who then, roughly 5,000 years ago, put it into written form for the benefit of modern man. (Prior to the modern age, according to the Vedic texts, man had a superb memory and did not require the written word.) Originally the Vedas existed as one exceedingly lengthy work. Vyasa, to make this knowledge accessible, divided it into four books, called Samhitas. These are the *Rig Veda* (the earliest sacred hymns of the Vedas), the *Sama Veda* (the Veda of melodies), the *Yajur Veda* (the Veda of rituals), and the *Atharva Veda* (the Veda of incantations). Vedic literature also includes explanatory books known as Brahmanas (treatises dealing with the technicalities of sacrifices) and Aranyakas (treatises for renunciants who go off into the wilderness to fulfill vows).

Also included is the vast storehouse of Upanishadic literature, philosophical texts meant to elucidate Vedic concepts. In addition, there are numerous Sutras (books of concise truths), such as the *Vedanta-sutras*, the *Shrauta-sutras*, the *Grihya-sutras*, the *Dharma-sutras*, and the *Shulba-sutras*. The Vedangas (auxiliary sciences connected with Vedic study) are also important: *shiksha* (phonetics), *chandas* (meter), *vyakarana* (grammar), *nirukta* (etymology), and *jyotish*

(astronomy/astrology). So, too, are the Upavedas (sciences not directly related to Vedic study): *Ayurveda* (the study of holistic medicine), *Gandharva-veda* (the study of music and dance), *Dhanur-veda* (military science), and *Sthapatya-veda* (architecture). Theologically most important are the many Puranas (such as the *Bhagavat Purana*) as well as the epics (like the *Mahabharata*—which includes the *Bhagavad-gita*—and the *Ramayana*). The many writings of *acharyas* ("enlightened teach-ers") should also be included in the Vedic literature, since they bring out the essence of earlier Vedic works and are thus considered "Vedic" in a practical sense.

The verses in each of the thousands of Vedic texts conform to strict rules of poetry and meter, and contain information on varied topics: from medicine and farming to a description or explanation of time sequences on upper and lower planets; from techniques of yoga and meditation to household hints and recipes for vegetarian dishes; from detailed explanations of governmental organization to masterful directions on construction and decoration of temples or residential buildings. The Vedas contain drama, history, and complex philosophy, as well as simple lessons of etiquette, military protocol, and the use of musical instruments. Most significantly, however, is that the Vedic literature explains both *rasa* ("relationship with God," or "the intense pleasure that comes from a distinct relation with the Supreme") and *bhakti* ("devotional love") in minute detail, as a science.

DIVISION OF SCRIPTURES

1. Shruti (revealed writings of "that which is heard"):
- The four Vedic Samhitas: *Rig, Sama, Yajur,* and *Atharva*
- Brahmanas
- Aranyakas
- Upanishads (of which there are more than 108 separate books)

2. Smriti (tradition, or "that which is remembered")
- Itihasas (epics) such as the *Ramayana* and the *Mahabharata* (which includes the *Bhagavad-gita*)
- Puranas, such as the eighteen prominent Mahapuranas:
  Six sattvik Puranas:
  Vishnu Purana
  Naradiya Purana
  Bhagavat Purana
  Garuda Purana
  Padma Purana
  Varaha Purana
  Six rajasik Puranas:
  Brahma Purana
  Brahmanda Purana
  Brahma-vaivarta Purana
  Markandeya Purana
  Bhavishya Purana
  Vamana Purana
  Six tamasik Puranas:
  Matsya Purana
  Kurma Purana
  Linga Purana
  Shiva Purana
  Skanda Purana
  Agni Purana
- Eighteen Upapuranas and numerous *sthala* (regional) Puranas
- Versified equivalents of the *Dharma-sutras: Manu-smriti, Vishnu-smriti,* etc.

3. Sutras (aphorisms)
- Shrauta-sutras, Grihya-sutras, Dharma-sutras, Shulba-sutras, Vedanta-sutras, etc.

4. Other categories include the Vedangas, the Upavedas, and the writings and commentaries of the great *acharyas* throughout history.

SHRIMAD BHAGAVATAM

The *Shrimad Bhagavatam (Bhagavata Purana)*, or simply the *Bhagavatam*, has often been called the Bible of the Vaishnavas. A vast and encyclopedic work, the *Bhagavatam* surveys a broad spectrum of knowledge, including history, psychology, politics, cosmology, metaphysics, and theology. The 19th-century American transcendentalist Ralph Waldo Emerson once exalted the *Bhagavatam* as a book to be read "on one's knees."

Vaisnavas teach that the profound revelation of the *Bhagavatam* was originally given by God to Brahma, the first created being, at the dawn of creation. Brahma conveyed the essence of this knowledge to Narada, and Narada passed it on to Vyasa, the compiler of the Vedic literature. Vyasa's place in the historical dissemination of "primordial knowledge" is significant. He is said to have divided the eternal wisdom of the Veda into four distinct sections. He then summarized the essence of Vedic knowledge into aphorisms known as the *Vedanta-sutras*. Vyasa, however, felt some despondency—in his entire compilation and summarization of the Vedic literature, he had neglected to focus truly on the personal feature of the Absolute Truth. This was confirmed by his spiritual master, Narada, who told him that he (Vyasa) would be satisfied only if he would directly describe the name, fame, form, and activities of Krishna, the Personality of Godhead. Heeding the advice of his guru, Vyasa compiled the *Shrimad Bhagavatam*—the "mature fruit of the Vedic tree of knowledge,"

Vyasadeva dictates the Shrimad Bhagavatam to his scribe, Ganesh.

Shri Chaitanya Mahaprabhu.

the "king of books," the "spotless Purana"—as a natural commentary on the *Vedanta-sutras*.

There were three subsequent retellings that enhanced the sweet flavor of the *Bhagavatam*. The first of these occurred at Badarikashrama, high in the Himalayas. Vyasa was the speaker, and his son, Shukadeva, was the chief recipient. The second time the *Bhagavatam* was recited, Shukadeva was the speaker. Adding to what he had heard from his father, he recited the *Bhagavatam* to Maharaj Parikshit, a great king who had been cursed to die within seven days. Finally, the third retelling of the *Bhagavatam* took place in the forest of Naimisharanya (on the banks of the Gomati at modern Nimsar in Uttar Pradesh). Here, 60,000 sages, headed by the saint Shri Shaunaka Rishi, assembled to hear the knowledge of the *Bhagavatam* from Suta Goswami, a sage who had listened well when Shukadeva revealed the *Bhagavatam* to Maharaj Parikshit. It is the sum total of these three revelations that make up the *Bhagavatam* as we know it today.

No other Purana has been summarized in as many forms or commented upon with such vitality. In addition to Shridhara Swami, one of its most important commentators, Viraraghava Acharya wrote a significant commentary on it too.

Sanatan Goswami, one of Shri Chaitanya's most distinguished followers, is said to have studied the *Bhagavatam* before meeting his master. However, after learning the sacred text from Mahaprabhu personally, he wrote one of his most memorable works, the *Brihad Bhagavatamrita*, a condensation of the entire *Bhagavatam* in story form. Other works by Rupa Goswami and Jiva Goswami, Sanatan's illustrious successors, also focus on the *Bhagavatam*. Most recently, the exhaustive commentary of A.C. Bhaktivedanta Swami Prabhupada has made the *Bhagavatam* clear and accessible for the modern world.

The Shrimad Bhagavatam *in English, translated and commentated on by His Divine Grace A. C. Bhaktivedanta Swami Prabhupada.*

THE BHAGAVATAM
ITS CONTENTS

The *Bhagavatam* asserts its unique nature at the very beginning of its pages: *dharmah projjhita-kaitavo 'tra*, "All religiosity covered by fruitive intentions is completely rejected herein." (1.1.2) The commentators define "fruitive intentions" as *kama* (gross and subtle sense gratification), *artha* (economic development), *dharma* (ordinary religiosity), and *moksha* (liberation). Thus, the *Bhagavatam* maintains that true religion, which centers on *bhakti*—devotion to Krishna—transcends mundane goals, noble as those goals may be. The *Bhagavatam* focuses exclusively on the ultimate goal of life: love of God.

The primary themes of the *Bhagavatam* are *sambandha* (man's relationship with God), *abhideya* (the process of awakening that relationship), and *prayojana* (the goal of that relationship).

The *Bhagavatam* elucidates these themes through a complex revelation that weaves throughout the traditional ten subjects of Puranic literature: **1.** *Sarga*, the primary creation, in which earth, water, fire, air, and ether, as well as the total material energy (or the Universal Form of God), come into being. **2.** *Visarga*, the secondary creation, or the work of Brahma, the first created being. **3.** *Sthana*, the way in which the Lord maintains the universe by His multifarious potencies, with detailed descriptions of His energies. **4.** *Poshana*, the reciprocal relationship between God and His devotee, and the practices designed to promote that relationship. **5.** *Uti*, a description of the conditioned soul's impulses for material activities. **6.** *Manvantara*, the scriptural instructions given to the living beings of this world. **7.** *Ishanukatha*, detailed information about the Personality of Godhead in His various forms. **8.** *Nirodha*, or the winding up of all energies in creation. God's potencies are described with special attention to the destruction of the material universe. **9.** *Mukti*, or the different kinds of liberation, from the cessation of material miseries to perfection in love of God. **10.** *Ashraya*, the ultimate end of knowledge: the transcendence. The Godhead is described in full, the activities of Krishna being the crown jewels of the *Bhagavatam's* brilliance.

ᵀᴴᴱ MAHABHARATA

As an epic of immense proportions—both in terms of length and content—the *Mahabharata* has become the basis of Indian myth, religion, and philosophical thought. It is composed of 110,000 Sanskrit couplets and is thus seven times the length of the *Iliad* and the *Odyssey* combined, or nearly three times the size of the Judeo-Christian Bible. Regarded by many to be as authoritative as the Vedas, the *Mahabharata* is known as "the fifth Veda." Vaishnavas regard it as an *itihasa*, or "history."

In its voluminous pages, the *Mahabharata* deals with a host of subjects, but the central narration focuses on the quarrel between the Pandavas and the Kauravas, two groups of cousins. The quarrel escalates into a full-scale civil war involving gods and men, tricksters and ascetics with magical powers, and *brahmanas* and royalty, and it ultimately jeopardizes the fate of the entire universe.

The *Mahabharata* has traditionally been interpreted in three distinct ways. Externally, it is the story of a particular royal family that becomes involved in a fierce fratricidal war. Even on this seemingly superficial level, the *Mahabharata* elucidates such qualities as heroism, courage, and saintliness. On the ethical plane, the war is seen as the perennial conflict fought in daily life between good and evil, justice and injustice, right and wrong—essentially, *dharma* against *adharma*.

On the spiritual level, the *Mahabharata* focuses on the battle between the higher self and the lower self, the war between man's spiritual calling and the dictates of the body, mind, and senses. The Vaishnava tradition views the *Mahabharata* as encompassing all three levels of reality, and the tradition offers guidance for each.

Lord Krishna, the divine charioteer, instructs Arjuna, His disciple and loving devotee.

THE BHAGAVAD GITA

Gita means "song," and *bhagavad* refers to "God, the possessor (*vat*) of all opulence (*bhaga*)." The *Bhagavad-gita*, therefore, is "The Song of the All-Opulent One"; it embodies the teachings of Lord Krishna.

The work comes to us in the form of dialogue between Lord Shri Krishna and the princely warrior Arjuna just before the onset of the devastating *Mahabharata* war.

Arjuna, putting aside his duty as a *kshatriya* (warrior), decides not to fight. This decision is motivated by personal considerations: his kinsmen and teachers are in the opposing army.

Krishna, who has agreed to become the driver of Arjuna's chariot, sees His friend and devotee in illusion, paralyzed by the fear that he must kill his relatives and friends. Feeling compassion, Krishna eloquently reminds Arjuna of his immediate social duty (*varna-dharma*) as a warrior upon whom people are depending, and, more importantly, of his religious duty (*sanatan-dharma*) as an eternal spiritual entity in relationship with God. The relevance and universality of Krishna's teachings transcend the immediate historical setting of Arjuna's battlefield dilemma.

The dialogue moves through a series of questions and answers that elucidate metaphysical concepts such as the distinction between body/soul (matter/spirit), the principle of nonattached action, the virtues of discipline (*yoga*) and meditation, and the place of knowledge (*gyana*) and devotion (*bhakti*). Krishna teaches that perfection lies not in renunciation of the world, but rather in disciplined action (*karma-yoga*), performed without attachment to results (*karma-phala-tyaga*).

Krishna shows Arjuna His Universal Form, which includes everything in existence, then His mystical four-armed Vishnu form, and finally His original two-armed form. He explains His many manifestations, such as Brahman, Paramatma, and Bhagavan (see later section on this subject), and ultimately reveals that His personal feature supersedes His impersonal aspects.

Krishna explains the three modes of material nature—goodness, passion, and ignorance—showing how an understanding of these three qualities, along with knowledge of the divine and demoniac natures, can lead to enlightenment. He explains the different kinds of liberation and the ultimacy of surrendering to Him with a heart of devotion.

WHAT IS DHARMA?

Although many scholars agree that "duty" is an acceptable translation of the Sanskrit *dharma,* the term is difficult to translate. It is used to refer to religion, ordinary religiosity, sacred duty, virtue, cosmic order, and so on. Etymologically, it derives from the verbal root *dhri,* which means "to hold," and more specifically, "that which holds everything together." Things are held together by their essential qualities. *Dharma* is consequently seen as "the essence of a given thing," or "a thing's inherent nature." The *dharma* of water is wetness. The *dharma* of honey is sweetness. And, according to the *Bhagavad-gita* the *dharma* of the soul is service to Krishna in love and devotion.

GITA COMMENTARIES

Although widely published and read as a separate text, originally the *Bhagavad-gita* appears as an episode in the sixth book of the *Mahabharata* (*Bhishma-parva*, chapters 23–40). It consists of 700 verses in eighteen chapters and is often referred to as the "Gitopanishad," in that it follows the style and philosophical conclusions of the Upanishads.

The *Gita's* depth of wisdom has inspired numerous commentaries; the *Gita* is said to be the most commented-upon book in the religious history of man. In India, practically every major teacher, dating back to antiquity, has contributed a commentary on the *Gita*. And the *Mahabharata* has its own built-in explanation of the *Gita*, because Book Fourteen (called the *Anugita*) is basically a summarization of the *Gita's* contents.

Long-established Vaishnava texts, such as the *Varaha Purana* and the *Padma Purana*, include a *Gitamahatmya* (verses

glorifying the *Gita*), and these are used by all schools of Indian thought. In the 7th and 8th centuries C.E., teachers of the impersonalistic school, such as Bhaskara and Shankara, wrote what are now considered classic Gita commentaries as well, though such works lack the personalistic insights of the Vaisnavas.

Most important are the many highly theistic commentaries that followed, particularly that of Shrila A.C. Bhaktivedanta Swami Prabhupada.

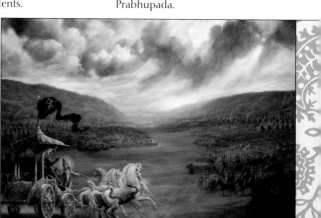

After the *Gita* was translated into English for the first time (by Charles Wilkins in 1785), its popularity began to soar outside India. Intellectuals among the Germans (Schlegel, Deussen, and Schopenhauer), Americans (Emerson and Thoreau), Englishmen (Max Mueller, who was English by adoption, and Aldous Huxley), Frenchmen (Romain Rolland), and Russians (Tolstoy) were greatly intrigued by the *Gita's* message. This message continues to be expounded upon even today.

"Of the sacred books of the Hindus, the *Bhagavad-gita* is the most widely read and probably the most important text for the understanding of Eastern mysticism."

—*R. C. Zaehner, University of Oxford*

RAMAYANA

The other great Sanskrit epic—the story of Rama—dates back to Treta Yuga, about two million years ago. The sage Valmiki was the first to compile it into written form. His version, known as the *Ramayana* ("The Path of Rama"), is still considered one of the two most important epics in Indian history (the other is the *Mahabharata*). It also has the distinction of being called the first poem (*adikavya*) within the storehouse of Sanskrit literature.

The *Ramayana* is often relished for its sheer beauty: beauty in terms of Sanskrit poetry, evocative visualization, and profound dialogue; beauty in terms of the morals and ethics invoked; beauty in terms of *dharma* (the importance of doing one's duty); beauty in terms of emotions brought to the fore; and perhaps most of all, beauty in terms of the persons depicted.

Chief among these persons is Rama Himself. Clearly described as an *avatar* ("God on earth"), Rama is tall, strong, and righteous. He is the embodiment of virtue, a true hero, who is not afraid to show His more "human" side: to love and to feel pain in separation when the woman so close to His heart is taken away from Him.

Sita, the woman in question, is also virtuous; she is the paradigm of chastity and all that is good and true. Lakshman, Rama's noble brother, selflessly serves the divine couple in all their needs. Finally, Hanuman, the half-man/half-monkey devotee

THE HIDDEN GLORY OF INDIA

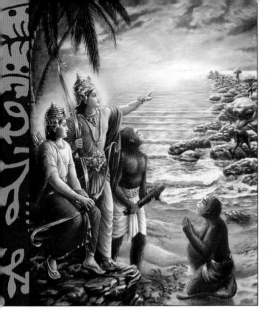

with Rama's ring as evidence of their alliance. In the *Yuddha-khanda*, the long-awaited battle between Rama's army and that of Ravana takes place. Rama is victorious and establishes the ideal God-centered kingdom, known in Indic tradition as Rama Rajya. The seventh book (*Uttara-khanda*) is generally considered an addendum. Here, Rama's two sons, Kusha and Lava, are born to Sita in Valmiki's hermitage, to which she had been banished by Rama after He heard rumors of her infidelity. Eventually Kusha and Lava are established on the throne of Ayodhya. But Sita, broken at her banishment, merges into the earth, and the remorseful Rama departs for His celestial abode.

of Rama, is the very emblem of strength, chivalry, loyalty, and devotion.

The first book of Valmiki's *Ramayana* (*Bala-khanda*) relates the divine birth of Rama, His childhood, and His marriage to Sita. In the second book (*Ayodhya-khanda*), Valmiki narrates the preparations for the coronation of Rama and the intrigue that leads to Rama's forest exile. The third book (*Aranya-khanda*) describes the forest life of Rama, Sita, and Lakshman, the personalities they meet, and the kidnapping of Sita. In the fourth book (*Kishkindha-khanda*), Rama meets Hanuman and Sugriva, forges a deep-rooted alliance with them, and coronates Sugriva as king of Kishkindha. Meanwhile Sugriva's elder brother Valin is killed and the mission of finding Sita gets underway. The fifth book (*Sundara-khanda*) elaborates on the personality and *lila* of Hanuman, who manages to find Sita and give her a message from Rama along

RAMA RETELLINGS

VARIATIONS ON A THEME

The *Ramayana* of Valmiki is generally considered the earliest and most authentic version of Rama's life. Variations on the original soon developed as the story was retold in the vernacular languages of each particular region of India.

Aside from the text of Valmiki, an early Sanskrit version of the Rama story is found in the *Mahabharata*, where a sage narrates to Yudhisthira the basic exploits of Rama. This section, called the *Ramopakhyana*, occurs in the *Aryana-parva*, or the Third Book of the *Mahabharata*. Another early Sanskrit version is found in the *Harivamsha*, which is appended to the *Mahabharata* and describes the life of Krishna. The ninth canto of the *Bhagavatam* also includes a brief description of Rama's adventures.

Variations on Rama's life can be found also in many other major Puranas. Through these the tale traveled to South India, where in the 11th century a sage named Kampan rewrote the *Ramayana* in Tamil. This work, which is considered the first vernacular *Ramayana*, is known as the *Iramavataram*. Kampan's retelling of the epic was followed by a Telugu version in the 13th century, and a Bengali one in the 14th.

With the medieval renaissance of *bhakti*, the 16th century brought forth many new *Ramayanas*, most notably the Sanskrit *Adhyatma-ramayana* (the "esoteric" *Ramayana*), thought to be composed in South India. This work offers a mystical reading of the story, with inventive allegories and intricate symbolism. Two other important versions are the *Ananda-ramayana* and the *Bhushundi-ramayana*. The latter work is so closely modeled after the *Bhagavata Purana* that it has often been called the *Rama-bhagavata*. But the most famous vernacular version is Tulsidas's *Ramcharitmanas*, written in Hindi also in the 16th century. It should be noted here that all these vernacular versions

are not merely translations of the *Ramayana* of Valmiki—they are usually entirely new books, loosely based on Valmiki but incorporating new insights, legends, and local lore. Yet, although most people know the story primarily through a regional account, all hold Valmiki's verses as particularly sacred.

The *Ramayana*, moreover, has a vast audience all over the world.

Called the *Ramakien* in Thailand, the *Serat Rama* in Indonesia, the *Yama Pwe* in Burma, and the *Maharadia Lawana* in the Philippines, it is conveyed through music and mime, poetry and popular folk tales, dramatic performances and video, comic books and epic narrations. The stories and personalities associated with the *lila* of Rama have captured the hearts of over one billion people worldwide.

Rama kills the evil Ravana.

"In view of the great popularity of Hatha-Yoga in the West, other fine forms or branches of Yoga have become eclipsed. Among them is Bhakti-Yoga, which has a far longer history than the Yoga of "force" (*hatha*). In fact, the path of devotion (*bhakti*) has its roots in the mystical ritualism of the ancient Vedas. These archaic Sanskrit scriptures are now thought to be well over four thousand years old."

— Georg Feuerstein, Ph.D.
Founder-director of the Yoga Research and Education Center (YREC)

VAISHNAVA ROOTS

2

EARLY
VAISHNAVISM
SOUTHERN ROOTS

Centuries after Vyasa compiled the Vedic literature, several great teachers did much to systematize the Vaishnava tradition. This occurred in both southern and northern provinces, with distinct features in each.

"There are any number of scriptural, literary, architectural, and archeological evidences for the antiquity of bhakti (Vaishnavism). But if we view the Indian religious history over the past two or three thousand years, it becomes apparent that bhakti tradition was strongest and most widespread in the medieval centuries—let's say from the eleventh century onward, beginning with the appearance of the great Vaishnava acharyas (spiritual teachers) like Ramanuja and Madhva. Many ancient bhakti strains crystallized into the medieval bhakti movement."

—Shrivatsa Goswami
Founder and director, Shree Chaitanya
Prema Sansthana, Vrindavan

A traditional story personifies *bhakti*, or devotional love, as a beautiful woman. Bhakti is born in Southern India and grows to maturity in due course. As the metaphor develops, Bhakti travels throughout India but reaches her greatness in the North. Indeed, the earliest evidence of Vaishnava culture is found in the South.

Southern Vaishnavism developed through the work of the Alvars, important early teachers of *bhakti*. Alvar means "absorbed in meditation" or "drenched in God." Such was indeed the mood of the saints and sages of the medieval *bhakti* movement in the South. There are twelve famous Alvars, but the most important are Nammalvar, Kulashekharalvar, and Andal (the daughter of Periyalvar). Their lives and poetry are remembered and savored by South Indian Vaishnavas, especially those belonging to the Ramanuja school.

Tradition usually ascribes prehistoric dates to the Alvars, asserting that they lived about five or six thousand years ago. According to most scholars of Indian religion, however, the Alvars lived some time between the 8th and 9th centuries (c.e.).

The Alvars composed the *Divya Prabandham*, a collection of four thousand devotional songs in Tamil. The South Indian Vaishnavas regard the *Divya Prabandham* as sacred, on a par with the Vedas, and in fact revere it as "the Vaishnava Veda".

The special feature of the *bhakti* religion as preached by the Alvars was its accessibility to people of high

A Ramanujite
sadhu in the line
of the Alvars.

and low castes, men and women,
rich and poor, wise and ignorant,
pious and impious alike. Among the
Alvars themselves, Andal was a
woman, Kulashekhara was a king
(the royal class were often thought
too engrossed in material affairs to
practice the Vaishnava religion seriously), and Tondaradippodi was a
reformed miscreant. The only thing
necessary for realization, according
to the Alvars, was *prapatti*, or surrender of the heart to God.

The songs of the Alvars have
been a great source of inspiration to
Vaishnavas throughout South India.
These songs may have influenced
Vaishnavism in the North as well,
since they taught the basic premise
of *rasa* ("relationship with God") that
was soon to be developed into a
science by the followers of Shri
Chaitanya.

The Alvars emphasized the *rasas* of
dasya (a servant's love for his master),
sakhya (friendly love), and *vatsalya*
(parental love).

They pursued also the *rasa* of
madhurya (conjugal love), but it was
really Shri Chaitanya who brought
out its special nectar. With a few
exceptions, the higher *rasas* were
rarely expressed in Alvar spirituality.

While the devotion of the Alvars
was thriving in the South, much of
North India, besieged by foreign
rule, had moved away from its
Vaishnava heritage. However, with
the appearance of a succession of
teachers that culminated in the
15th century with Shri
Chaitanya Mahaprabhu,
this was all to change.

A South Indian temple
like those in which the
Alvars worshiped.

eARLY
VAISHNAVISM
NORTHERN ROOTS

According to the previously mentioned metaphor, Bhakti was born in the South. A good deal of archeological evidence shows, however, that Bhakti also had a twin born in the northern provinces.

Books such as Suvira Jaiswal's *The Origin and Development of Vaishnavism* (Delhi: Munshiram Manoharlal, 1967) and R.P. Chanda's *Archaeology and the Vaishnava Tradition* (Memoirs of the Archaeological Survey of India No. 5, 1920) have conclusively established the early existence of North Indian Vaishnavism.

Still, it was not until the 12th century that *bhakti* movements became a major force in northern and central India, from Kashmir and Gujarat to Bengal and Orissa. At this time, a gifted generation of practitioners composed poems that would define the Vaishnava tradition by expressing themes from traditional scriptures, such as the *Shrimad Bhagavatam* and *Bhagavad-gita*, in vernacular languages. Yale scholar Richard Davis writes of the depth and devotion of North Indian *bhakti* poetry:

"In contrast to Indian courtly traditions of poetic composition, poet-saints of North India sang in vernacular languages and drew their imagery from everyday life. They adopted highly personal poetic voices to speak of the tribulations and joys of devotional life. The poetry of medieval bhakti in Hindi, Bengali, Marathi, and other vernacular languages of India is quite likely the richest library of devotion in world literature, distinguished not only by its religious intensity but also by the great variety of psychological states and emotional responses it explores. These medieval songs of devotion remain very much alive in contemporary India. Few of us indeed can recite as much of any author as the average Hindi speaker can reel off from Kabir, Surdas, or Mirabai."[1]

Three North Indian writers—
Vidyapati, Jayadeva, and
Chandidas—among others, added
to the fervor by producing a
body of particularly profound
poetry. These poets and saints
emphasized the intensity of love
of God in separation—a form of
spiritual longing rarely achieved.
Expressing the deeper sentiments
of Vaishnava mysticism, their
work greatly influenced later
teachers. Formal systematization
of northern Vaishnava thought
was eventually effected by several
prominent teachers, most notably by
Vallabha, Shri Chaitanya, and the Six
Goswamis of Vrindavan.

Notes

1. *Donald S. Lopez, ed. 1995. "Religions of India
   in Practice," 40. Princeton University Press.*

BUDDHA & SHANKARA

According to Vaishnava history, the majority of India strictly followed the Vedic tradition until the time of Buddha (500 B.C.E.). By that time there was rampant misinterpretation of Vedic texts. This resulted in the performance of outdated sacrifices (meant for previous ages) and in these sacrifices the slaughter of animals.

To remedy the situation, Buddha found that he had to repudiate the Vedas in toto. Rather than address metaphysical dimensions of reality as the Vedas do, he was concerned with morals, ethics, principles of psychological empowerment, the nature of suffering, and how to overcome suffering. He taught the law of impermanence, that is to say, he elaborated on the temporary nature of everything material and on the law of causation, i.e., that nothing happens by chance.

Buddha taught that the best way to live in such a world was to follow the Middle Way. This evokes a balanced, harmonious view of life without the extremes of either self-indulgence or severe asceti-cism. The Four Noble Truths, which lay at the basis of Buddhist thought, state that (1) suffering is universal, (2) suffering is caused by desire or craving, (3) suffering can be prevented or overcome, and (4) the principles of Buddhism embody the way to remove suffering. These principles can be summarized as the Eightfold Path: right conduct, right motive, right resolve, right speech, right livelihood, right attention, right effort, and right meditation on behaving in a good way.

Buddhism, then, basically carries a pre-theistic message: "Purify your thoughts and be a good person; by doing this, you will rise beyond material suffering." Consequently, Buddhism does not discuss God or earlier Vedic teachings.

In the 8th century C.E., however, Shankara, an incarnation of Lord Shiva, appeared. He reestablished the Vedic scrip-tures, albeit in a slightly altered form. Shankara taught that the Vedas were divinely inspired but were to be interpreted in a metaphorical and, ultimately, impersonalistic way. In other words, for Shankara, God was primarily an abstract force, and any personal reference to God in the scriptures was to be taken either in a symbolic sense or as a statement of God's lesser nature. This appealed to Shankara's predominantly Buddhist audience, who were trained to think in terms of abstract philosophy and psychology, and not in terms of recognizing a Supreme Being.

In summary, Buddha's appearance in this world served the function of distracting people from the Vedic texts because people were misinterpreting those texts, and Shankara served the purpose of reestablishing the Vedas in a way that Buddhists could appreciate. According to Vaishnavas, this was part of a divine plan to reinstate Vedic culture. This reinstatement began to occur by the 11th century, with the appearance of Ramanujacharya.

Above: Buddha in meditation.

Right: Shankara, the teacher of impersonalism.

SIDDHARTHA GAUTAMA

Vaishnavas accept Buddha (whose birth name was Siddhartha Gautama) as an incarnation of Vishnu. The *Shrimad Bhagavatam* (1.3.24), which predicts his appearance 2,500 years before he was born, states that he would take birth in the province of Gaya and that his mother's name would be Anjana. Historically, however, Siddhartha Gautama was not born in Gaya but in Nepal. It was his enlightenment that occurred in Gaya. In other words, "Siddhartha" may have been born in Nepal, but "Buddha" was born in Gaya.

Similarly, history relates that Buddha's mother was known as Mayadevi, not Anjana. Nonetheless, it was his grandmother, Anjana, who raised Buddha from the moment his mother passed away, six days after his birth. Thus, effectively, Anjana was his mother.

In this way, the *Bhagavatam* gives an inner reading on the life of Buddha. According to the poet Jayadeva Goswami, Buddha's hidden mission was not to found Buddhism per se; his purpose, rather, was to put an end to needless violence and animal sacrifices.

ACHARYAS
GREAT MASTERS

The teachings of Shankara were challenged by the great devotional preaching of the Alvars, which culminated in the appearance of Ramanuja (1017–1137). He took the Vedic restoration one step further. Whereas Buddha denied the scriptures altogether, and Shankara reinstated them but in an impersonalistic way, Ramanuja moved closer to the original monotheism of the Vedas by formulating his Vishishtadvaita philosophy—a sort of qualified monism. "We are the same as God," Ramanuja taught, "but we are different as well." To many followers of Shankara, it seemed that Ramanuja accentuated the similarity rather than the difference, and this allowed his thought to enter a predominantly Shankarite milieu.

In Ramanuja we see the dawning of the actual Vaishnava *siddhanta* (conclusion)—taking truth a step further than either Buddha or Shankara. This is so because he ultimately acknowledged the distinction between the living entity and God. Whereas Shankara denied this distinction, claiming that the living being is one with God, Ramanuja detected it. It was Madhva who went further, to the point of emphasizing our distinction from God.

Approximately one hundred years after the time of Ramanuja, Madhva (1239–1319) preached his doctrine of Dvaita, clearly accentuating the dual nature of reality—there is God, and there is the living entity, and the two are never one. Historically, Indian philosophical literature has largely been an ongoing exposition of the differences between Madhva's school of pure dualism, Ramanuja's qualified monism, and the monistic school of Shankara. Madhvacharya took an uncompromising position. He would not hear of any similarity between God and the finite soul. His Vaishnavism even today stands as a strong protest to the atheism of Buddhism and the monism of Shankara.

To summarize: Shankara denied the distinction between God and the living entity, Ramanuja recognized it, and Madhva emphasized it. With Shri Chaitanya's appearance, according to the Gaudiya Vaishnavas, the final part of the Vedic restoration took place: Shri

Shri Chaitanya
(1486–1533)

Madhva
(1239–1319)

Ramanuja
(1017–1137)

Chaitanya harmonized the oneness and difference between God and the living entity. His teaching became known as Acintya-bhedabheda-tattva, or "the inconceivable and simultaneous oneness with and difference from God." We are one with God in quality, Shri Chaitanya taught, but not in quantity. A drop of water and an entire ocean, chemically analyzed, are exactly the same. But one is small and the other is great.

Similarly, God is full of all opulences, such as beauty, wealth,

fame, knowledge, strength, and renunciation. The living entity, as a part of God, has these qualities as well, but in minute proportion. Therefore, the living entity is not supreme. Rather, being subservient, he is meant to serve the Supreme. This was the original Vedic teaching, gradually reestablished through a long historical revelation involving Vyasa, Buddha, Shankara, Ramanuja, Madhva, and, finally, Shri Chaitanya Mahaprabhu. There were many other great *acharyas* as well, such as Nimbarka, Vallabha, and Vishnuswami, but the six teachers mentioned above are most important in understanding the historical unfolding of Vedic knowledge. This unfolding enhanced the Vaishnavism of the South and reestablished the rich tradition of the North.

THE GODHEAD

Godhead is light. Nescience is darkness.
Where there is Godhead, there is no nescience.
—*Vedic aphorism*

3 ASPECTS OF GOD

Indian theology recognizes three aspects of God: Brahman, **Paramatma**, and Bhagavan—the Lord's impersonal feature, His all-pervading localized aspect, and His supreme personhood. The three primary attributes of God—*sat* (being, or eternality), *chit* (full cognition), and *ananda* (unending bliss)—appear in these three aspects. *Sat* is realized in Brahman, *sat* and *chit* in Paramatma, and *sat*, *chit*, and *ananda* in Bhagavan. In Bhagavan, therefore, one realizes the sum total of all God's qualities.

BRAHMAN

Brahman realization (an understanding of God as an all-pervading universal force) is a fundamental view of God. This view is appealing to empiricists who are inclined to spiritual subjects. Those who take this conception more seriously undertake a mystical path called *gyana-yoga*, a traditional discipline that focuses on the intellect. By this path one can achieve full Brahman realization, or awareness of eternality (*sat*). Most current forms of yoga and religiosity, at their best, attempt to bring adherents to this basic spiritual perception. Persons who follow this path are known as *gyana-yogis*. Their quest for truth brings them to the Lord's effulgence, the impersonal Brahmajyoti, into which they may merge after death. There is a tendency, however, to fail in this pursuit, because the vast

The impersonal Brahman

impersonalism of eternality impels one to long for natural, interpersonal relationships. And so the practitioner may be born again to continue on the spiritual path.

PARAMATMA

A *gyana-yogi* may raise himself to the next level of realization and become an *ashtanga-yogi*, practicing the eightfold path of yoga as outlined in Patanjali's *Yoga-sutras*. If such a yogi is successful, he realizes the localized form of God, who is in every heart

His companion to give up the pursuit of temporary pleasures. This, of course, may take many lifetimes. But when the living being finally turns to the Supersoul in love and devotion, the Supersoul agrees to direct him. He brings the living being into association with a pure devotee, one who is accomplished in Bhagavan realization. When this occurs, one moves on to the final aspect of God consciousness.

BHAGAVAN

The word *Bhagavan* is the Sanskrit equivalent of "God." It literally means "He who possesses all opulences in full." The sages of the East have identified six primary opulences: strength, beauty, wealth, fame, knowledge, and renunciation. Only the Supreme Personality of Godhead has these qualities in full. One who becomes adept at worshiping Him becomes aware of eternity and knowledge— as in Brahman and Paramatma realization—and develops a profound sense of transcendental bliss (*ananda*) as well. The person on the path of Bhagavan realization attains intimacy with God, ultimately developing a loving relationship with him in a deep and meaningful way. Thus, Vaishnavism teaches that Bhagavan realization is the perfection of *gyana-yoga* and *ashtanga-yoga*, and, indeed, of all spiritual pursuits.

as well as within every atom. This manifestation of the Lord is called the Paramatma, or Supersoul. Upon realizing Him, one achieves awareness of more than immortality: one attains the essence of spiritual knowledge (*chit*) as well.

The Vaishnava *acharyas* explain the position of the Paramatma in the following way: As the sun may appear reflected in countless jewels, so the Lord within every atom may appear like many, though He is one, existing (in His original form) in the spiritual world.

An inherent danger in pursuing the path of the Paramatma is misidentification of one's individual soul with the Supersoul (Paramatma). To clarify this subject, the Vedic literature gives the following analogy. The Supersoul and the individual soul are like two birds sitting in the same tree. The individual soul is enjoying the fruits of the tree, while the Supersoul stands by and watches, waiting for

Bhagavan Krishna,
the Supreme Lord.

3 ASPECTS:
an analogy

To make the three levels of God-realization more understandable, later Vaishnava commentators have supplied the following apt analogy. Three simple villagers and their guide are at a railway station, waiting in great anticipation for the train to arrive. The three have never before seen a train. As one of them notices a massive structure pulling in at a distance, he comments on the headlight: "What is this?" he asks. The guide responds: "This is the train." Confident that he has seen the train, the first villager leaves, satisfied.

When the train approaches the platform, one of the remaining two villagers exclaims, "Oh! *This* is the train!" He has seen the series of cars pulling into the station—the form behind the headlights. He is now also confident that he has seen all there is to see, and leaves.

The third man patiently remains behind. And when the train comes into the station, he has the opportunity to meet the conductor and to see the various passengers on board.

The three villagers went back to their small village and began to tell everyone what they had seen. Though it was an undeniable truth that each had seen the same train, their descriptions were diverse; their realizations were different. The third villager obviously had a more complete experience than the other two. He was able to convince the others of this, for he perfectly described what his two comrades had seen, and more.

Analogically, the big light represents the effulgent impersonal aspect of the Lord (Brahman). This light with something more concrete behind it conveys the idea of divine substance, a personality that pervades all existence (Paramatma). And

the third villager's vision represents the most complete aspect of God realization (Bhagavan), wherein one meets the Supreme Personality of Godhead, Lord Shri Krishna, and develops a relationship with Him.

Paramatma, the Supersoul.

In the Vaishnava view, these three are considered different aspects of the same Absolute Truth, and they are all valid. One views these different aspects of God according to one's level of spiritual advancement. Vaishnava teachers recommend meditation on the fullest truth: Bhagavan realization. The other processes were developed for gradual elevation to this point. Under the direction of an elevated Vaishnava, however, one can immediately pursue the path of Bhagavan realization, surpassing the levels of Brahman and Paramatma.

Left: The impersonal aspect.

Right: Lord Krishna, ultimate Godhead, in all His glory.

SHRI KRISHNA

"The Supreme Lord, the embodiment of truth, consciousness, and joy, is known as Govinda, or Krishna. He is beginningless, the origin of everything, and the cause of all causes." (*Brahma-samhita* 5.1)

Krishna is Bhagavan, the Supreme Personality of Godhead. The *Shrimad Bhagavatam* (1.3.27), a scripture central to Vaishnava thought, reveals Krishna's identity: "Krishna is God Himself" (*krishnas tu bhagavan svayam*)—He is not merely a portion or manifestation of God, as are so many other divinities in India; He is the original Manifestor, the Complete Godhead. He displayed on earth His eternal *lila*, or spiritual activities, approximately 5,000 years ago. Vaishnava tradition teaches that Krishna engages in these activities eternally but manifested them on our planet only at that time.

Among Krishna's various pastimes, the following comprise the very essence of Indian culture: His birth in the prison of Kamsa, His playful and mischievous childhood activities as the son of Nanda and Yashoda, His killing of various demons, His dalliances with Shri Radha and the *gopis*, His heart-rending departure from Braj for Mathura, His regal activities in His kingdom in Dvaraka, His tryst with Radha at Kurukshetra, and His speaking of the *Bhagavad-gita*.

Several pastimes of Krishna reflect grandeur and even retribution, as when He rids the world of evil forces. Despite this, Krishna's appearance underscores the superiority of love over power, sweetness over opulence. While most concepts of God evoke feelings of awe and reverence, Krishna

KRISHNA'S DIVINITY IN BHAGAVAD-GITA

In the *Gita*, Krishna's status is clear: "I am the source of everything; from Me the entire creation flows." (10.8) "There is no truth superior to Me." (7.7) "By all the Vedas, I am to be known." (15.15)

Arjuna prays to Krishna, "You are the Supreme Brahman, the Ultimate, . . . the Absolute Truth, and the eternal Divine Person. You are the primal God, transcendental and original . . ." (10.12), "You are the original personality, the Godhead . . ." (11.38)

Throughout the *Gita*, Krishna is called Purushottama ("the Supreme Person"), Parabrahman ("the Supreme Brahman"), Adideva ("the original Lord"), Parameshvara ("the Supreme Controller"), and so on.

evokes intimacy and personal relationship. Vaishnava poets have suggested that His beautiful appearance—dark-bluish skin, large lotuslike eyes, and long raven-black hair adorned with a colorful peacock feather— seems to beckon the soul, to call out for interpersonal relationship. It is said that when one hears Krishna's flute, one cannot help but run to Him in a state of divine madness.

eXPANSIONS of KRISHNA

Krishna is Bhagavan (God), the source of all reality, but He has many other manifestations. He exists in various forms to accommodate the diverse sentiments of His devotees. Though Krishna is love personified, He also manifests Himself as Vishnu (Narayana), who is power and majesty personified. Vishnu further expands as the avatars (incarnations), such as Nrisimha, Vamana, Varaha, and Rama.

The supplementary Vedic texts afford considerable technical information about these expansions and incarnations. Krishna and His expansions are referred to as *svayam-rupa*, *tad-ekatma*, and *avesha*. Krishna's personal form (*svayam-rupa*) embodies His original, self-existent nature.

From this form comes His secondary manifestation (*tad-ekatma*), which is identical in essence to His original form but may differ in appearance and potency. In addition, He may manifest Himself as an especially empowered living being (*avesha*), such as Buddha or Jesus.

These three aspects of the Supreme expand further into subdivisions known as *vilasa* and *svamsha*, which in turn can be divided into *vaibhava* and *prabhava* expansions. In other words, Gaudiya-Vaishnava texts outline the many aspects of God in great detail.

Despite God's many manifestations, the scriptures say that "God is one" (*eka brahma dvitiya nasti*). This stands in contrast to the often-held view that Indian religion promulgates the worship of many gods. Given the intricacy of the tradition —especially regarding Krishna and His multitudinous expansions and incarnations—it becomes clear how such an oversimplified idea has arisen. However, a careful examination of the texts reveals a highly monotheistic tradition.

KEŚAVA

ACYUTA

HRṢĪKEŚA

NṚSIMHA

HARI

PADMANĀBHA

MADHUSŪDANA

ADHOKṢAJA

VĀ...

UPEN...

In addition to expanding into His various incarnations, Vishnu also expands into the innumerable universes and then into every atom.

AVATARS of VISHNU

As **Krishna** expands into His Vishnu **forms**, He also expands into unlimited kinds of avatars, each descending to accomplish a different mission. Of the many incarnations, ten figure most prominently in various texts.

The Lord "descends from His abode" (this is the root meaning of the word *avatar*) from age to age. At the dawn of creation, Vishnu incarnated as an aquatic known as Matsya Avatar—a divine fish that plunged into the depths of the ocean to recover the *Vedas*. He then appeared as a tortoise, Kurma, and played a vital role in the churning of the Milk Ocean. As the ages began to shift, the Lord appeared as a boar named Varaha and rescued the earth from the demon Hiranyaksha. As the half-man, half-lion Nrisimha He rescued His pure devotee, the little boy Prahlad, from the tyranny of Prahlad's evil father. He also became a dwarf *brahmana*, Vamana, who reclaimed the earth from a demon-king by an ingenious trick involving a mere "three steps of land"—three steps that engulfed the entire cosmos. He then manifested Himself as Parashuram, or "Rama-with-an-axe," and rid the world of merciless warriors. He also came as the celebrated Ramachandra and later appeared in His original form as Krishna, along with His immediate expansion Balaram, who appeared as His elder brother. Twenty-five hundred years ago He appeared as Buddha.

In the future, toward the end of Kali-yuga (in roughly 427,000 years), the Lord is predicted to appear as Kalki. At this time, He initiates the devastation of the material world and liberates the souls who remain at that time, taking them with him to his eternal kingdom. Vaishnava texts devote countless pages to descriptions of such *avatars*.

ПRISIMHA AVATAR

Perhaps the most fantastic and extraordinary-looking of Vishnu's avatars is Nrisimhadeva ("half-man, half-lion"). His story is intriguing.

many thousands of years ago, in a previous time cycle, when living entities lived for inordinate periods, a powerful tyrant king named Hiranyakashipu desired immortality. To achieve this goal, he performed severe penances for more than 36,000 years, hoping that the demigods would grant him eternal life.

The demigod Lord Brahma appeared before Hiranyakashipu to inform him that even he, Brahma, does not live forever, although he lives for trillions of years. Consequently, he was not able to grant eternal life to anyone.

The cunning Hiranyakashipu then requested: "If I cannot become immortal, then please grant me that I not be killed by any weapon known to men, nor killed on land or water or in the sky, nor indoors nor outdoors, nor in the daytime or at night." After securing these benedictions from Brahma, Hiranyakashipu felt confident that he had tricked Brahma and, in so doing, had achieved immortality.

Now Hiranyakashipu's only problem was his child Prahlad, the most pious of his four sons. Though Hiranyakashipu loved Prahlad, he could not tolerate the boy's penchant for serving Vishnu. Prahlad would teach all his schoolmates about devotional love. When Hiranyakashipu reprimanded him, Prahlad replied that people should be more interested in God than in materialistic pursuits.

This infuriated Hiranyakashipu, who was chief among the atheists. His love quickly turned to hate, and in various ways he arranged for his son to be killed. But in each case Prahlad was saved by divine intervention. Frustrated that Prahlad had managed to escape death, Hiranyakashipu decided to kill him with

*Hiranyakashipu attacks
Lord Nrisimhadeva.*

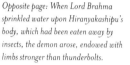

*Opposite page: When Lord Brahma
sprinkled water upon Hiranyakashipu's
body, which had been eaten away by
insects, the demon arose, endowed with
limbs stronger than thunderbolts.*

He lifted
Hiranyakashipu
onto His lap
and, ripping open
his abdomen,
disemboweled
the arrogant ruler.

his own hands. However, he first asked Prahlad one simple question: "How were you able to survive the attempts on your life? What is the source of your strength?"

Prahlad responded that everything occurs by the will of the Lord, and that the source of his strength is actually the source of all strength—God.

Now Hiranyakashipu's anger knew no bounds. He demanded to see this God that so occupied his son's attention. "Where is this Supreme Lord you always talk about?"

Prahlad answered that his Lord was all-pervading. "If He is everywhere," raged Hiranyakashipu, "then why is He not in this pillar?" And he pointed with his sword to a massive pillar where they stood. Upon striking the pillar with his fist, Hiranyakashipu was shocked to

see the pillar explode, revealing the immensely powerful form of Nrisimhadeva, the divine Man-Lion.

For a while Lord Nrisimha tolerated Hiranyakashipu's vain attempt to battle with Him, but then He lifted Hiranyakashipu onto His lap and, ripping open his abdomen, disemboweled the arrogant ruler.

Nrisimhadeva saved the planet from a merciless tyrant in such a way that all of Brahma's benedictions were honored: Hiranyakashipu was killed not by man or beast but by the Lord Himself—half-man, half-lion. He was killed neither on land nor in the sky but on the Lord's lap. He was killed neither indoors nor outside but in the doorway of an assembly hall. He was killed during neither day nor night but at twilight, and not with any weapon known to men but with the Lord's transcendental nails.

THE ORIGINAL GODDESS

Although Indian society is generally considered patriarchal, it does have an ancient tradition of Shaktism, or goddess worship. This is traceable to the ancient Veda, where the goddesses Ushas, Vak, Ratri, Aditi, Sarasvati, Prithivi, and other female divinities are described. As "Hinduism" developed, goddesses such as Parvati, Tara, Chinnamasta, the Mahavidyas, and the Matrikas became increasingly popular. This tendency culminated in the worship of a generic goddess known as Mahadevi, also called Durga, Kali, Uma, and so on, according to her various manifestations and the regions in which she is worshiped. She is the divine shakti (energy) of the universe.

from the Vaishnava point of view, this divine feminine energy (*shakti*) implies a divine source of energy (*shaktiman*). Thus, the goddess always has a male counterpart. Sita relates to Rama; Lakshmi belongs to Narayana; Radha has Her Krishna. As Krishna is the source of all manifestations of God, Shri Radha, His consort, is the source of all *shaktis*, or feminine

manifestations of cosmic energy. She is thus the original goddess.

Vaishnavism can be seen as a type of Shaktism wherein the *purna-shakti*, or the most complete form of the divine feminine energy, is worshiped as the preeminent aspect of divinity, eclipsing even the male Godhead in certain respects. For example, in Shrivaishnavism, Lakshmi (a primary expansion of Shri Radha) is

Radha, the original goddess, and Krishna.

her devotion and service to Krishna, she becomes the mediator of his grace (prasada, anugraha) and compassion (kripa). She is constituted of love for Krishna and is the main channel through which he sends his own love to his devotees. Thus she herself becomes a revered object of worship. As Krishna declares in the 'Brahmavaivarta Purana,' he will not grant moksha [liberation] to anyone who does not revere Radha; he even affirms that the worship of Radha is more pleasing to him than his own."[1]

Notes

1. *C. Mackenzie Brown. 1982. 'The Theology of Radha in the Puranas,' In Hawley and Wulff, eds., "The Divine Consort: Radha and the Goddesses of India,"69. Berkeley Religious Studies Series.*

considered the divine mediatrix, without whom access to Narayana is not possible. In the Gaudiya tradition, Radha is acknowledged as the Supreme Goddess, for it is said that She controls Krishna with Her love.

The supremacy of the original Goddess is summarized by C. Mackenzie Brown, associate professor of religion and chairman of the Asian Studies Department at Trinity University:

"Radha's…role is closely related to her status as Krishna's favorite. Through

The goddess Lakshmi, Shri Radha's first expansion.

Durga, the original goddess of this material world.

RADHA

"Essence of beauty and *rasa*,
Quintessence of bliss and compassion,
Embodiment of sweetness and brilliance,
Epitome of artfulness, graceful in love:
May my mind take refuge in Radha,
Quintessence of all essences."

— *Prabodhananda Sarasvati*

*"Radha's name is the greatest treasure.
Krishna plays that name on His flute,
remembering it constantly. She is the thread
in every fabric, each yantra and mantra,
each Veda and Tantra.
Shukadeva knew this secret of secrets,
but decided it best stay unrevealed;
Krishna incarnates to pursue it: still
its depth eludes even Him."*

— *Hariram Vyas*

In traditional Vaishnava literature, Krishna is compared to the sun, and Radha to the sunshine. Both exist simultaneously, but one comes from the other. Still, it is a misconception to say that the sun is prior to the sunshine—as soon as there is a sun, there is sunshine. More importantly, the sun has no meaning without sunshine, without heat and light. And heat and light would not exist without the sun. Thus, the sun and the sunshine co-exist, each equally important for the existence of the other. It may be said that they are simultaneously one and different.

Likewise, the relationship between Radha and Krishna is that of inconceivable identity in difference. They are, in essence, a single entity—God, who manifests as two distinct individuals for the sake of interpersonal exchange. As the tradition teaches, "Lord Krishna enchants the world, but Shri Radha enchants even Him. Therefore She is the supreme goddess of all. Shri Radha is the full power, and Lord Krishna is

"Lord Krishna enchants the world, but Shri Radha enchants even Him. Therefore She is the supreme goddess of all."

(Chaitanya-charitamrita, Adi-lila 4.95)

the possessor of full power. The two are not different, as evidenced by the revealed scriptures. They are indeed the same, just as musk and its scent are inseparable, or as fire and its heat are nondifferent. Thus, Radha and Krishna are one, although They have taken two forms to enjoy a relationship—this is Their mysterious *lila*." (*Chaitanya-charitamrita*, Adi-lila 4.95–98)

To increase the joy of relationship, Radha further expands into the many *gopis* of Braj. In the ancient Vaishnava texts, such as *Harivamsha* and some early Puranas, the individual *gopis* are not mentioned by name, though they are referred to as a group. Krishna is depicted as meeting with many cowherd girls at once. But in the *Bhagavatam* one sees that a special *gopi* emerges, particularly in the episode of the Rasa Dance. However, Shukadeva, the speaker of the *Bhagavatam*, does not mention Her by name. Gaudiya tradition asserts that this *gopi* is Radha (literally "She who satisfies Krishna most"). She and the other *gopis* are elaborately described in the *Naradiya*, *Padma*, and *Brahma-vaivarta Puranas* and in later literature. Radha's place in Vaishnava history, however, was not fully revealed until as late as the 12th century C.E., when Jayadeva Goswami and Nimbarkacharya wrote about Her

in their poetic treatises. In the writings of the Six Goswamis of Vrindavan, there is a wealth of information about the *gopis*, and preeminently about Radha.

In his *Stavavali* (15.1–10), Raghunath Das Goswami, the great mystical poet among the Six Goswamis of Vrindavan, describes Radha as if She were standing before him: "Radha makes even Lakshmi [the goddess of fortune] despair of her charms. Radha's inner silken garment is Her modesty. Her body is delicately painted with the saffron of beauty and the musk of glowing *shringara-rasa* [the amorous mood]. Her ornaments are fashioned from nine most precious jewels: Her trembling, tears, thrilling, stupor, perspiration, stammering, blushing, madness, and swoon. Her garland is prepared from the flowers of a select assortment of aesthetic qualities, and Her garment is freshened with the pure, subtle perfume of Her exquisite virtues. She reddens Her lips with the betel-leaf of intense attachment, and the guile of love is Her mascara. Her ears are perpetually adorned with glorious earrings—the sound of Krishna's name."

THE GOPIS: COWHERD MAIDENS of BRAJ

"The **energies** [consorts] of the Supreme Lord are of three kinds: the Lakshmis in Vaikuntha, the queens in Dvaraka, and the *gopis* in Vrindavan. The *gopis* are the best of all, for they have the privilege of serving Shri Krishna, the primeval Lord, the son of the **King of Braj**."

(Chaitanya-charitamrita, Adi-lila 1.79–80)

Shri Radha is the foremost of the *gopis*, able to please Krishna with Her mere glance. However, Radha feels that Her love for Krishna can always expand to greater heights. Therefore, She manifests Herself as the many *gopis* of Braj, who fulfill Krishna's desire for relationship (*rasa*) in a variety of ways.

The *gopis* are considered the *kaya-vyuha* of Shri Radha. There is no English equivalent for this term,

but it can be explained as follows: If one person could simultaneously exist in more than one human form at a single time, those forms would be known as the *kaya* ("body") *vyuha* ("multitude of") of that individual. In other words, these forms are one and the same person, but occupy different space and time and have different moods and emotions. As Radha and Krishna's sole purpose is to love each other, the *gopis* exist to assist Them in this love.

The *gopis* are divided into five groups, the most important group being the *parama-preshtha-sakhis* (the eight primary *gopis*). The *gopis* of that group are named Lalita, Vishakha, Chitra, Indulekha, Champakalata, Tungavidya, Rangadevi, and Sudevi. Many details of their lives

According to the Vaishnava scripture Bhakti Ratnakara, *the gopis so loved Krishna that they combined their bodies into the form of an elephant and allowed Him to ride upon them, to spare His lotus feet from the hot sands of Braj.*

Clearly, the tradition sees the love of the *gopis* as transcendental love of the highest order, countering any accusations of mundane sexuality, with clearly defined distinctions between lust and love. Like the Bride-of-Christ concept in the Christian tradition, and the Kabbalistic concept of the Feminine Divine in Jewish mysticism, "*gopi*-love" is theologically profound and constitutes the zenith of spiritual awareness. *Gopi*-love represents the purest love a soul may have for its

and services are described in esoteric scriptures, including their parents' names, their spouses' names, their skin color, ages, birthdays, moods, temperaments, favorite melodies, instruments, closest girlfriends, and so on. These elements form the substance of an inner meditation, or *sadhana*, which is designed to bring the devotee to the spiritual realm. Through such meditation one gradually develops *prema*, or love for Krishna.

divine source; the only correlation this love may have to mundane lust is in appearance alone.

TULASI DEVI

THE PLANT OF DEVOTION

Vaishnavism is an all-encompassing theistic sensibility that includes impersonalistic, pantheistic, panentheistic, and monotheistic ideas. It also includes a sense of animism, in which natural objects are seen as being imbued with the Divine. The foundation for this concept is the *Bhagavad-gita,* where Krishna describes Himself as the original fragrance of the earth, the light of the sun and the moon, the flower-bearing spring, the pure taste of water, and so on. The whole universe, in fact, is described as Krishna's Universal Form.

More directly, Mount Govardhan—a large land area that was at one time a formidable mountain—may be the most popular example of Krishna in the form of material nature. The pebbles and rocks of Govardhan, like the sacred stones known as Shalagram Shilas, are venerated by members of the Vaishnava community. These rock forms of Krishna are worshiped in intricate, detailed rituals. To the Vaishnava, this is a testimony to the Lord's accessibility.

Krishna's devotees sometimes incarnate in natural objects to gain proximity to Him. Tulasi is one such example. Tulasidevi, who is a plant manifestation[1] of Vrindadevi, the goddess of forests, comes into this world so that her leaves can be placed at Krishna's lotus feet. So deep is her attachment for Krishna that she is displeased if her leaves or twigs are placed at the feet of anyone else. Tulasi also incarnates as the purifying waters of the Gandaki River, whose stones are used for Shalagram worship.

Tulasi, in her form as Vrindadevi, is the embodiment of Lila-shakti, the Lord's "pastime" energy. She makes elaborate arrangements for the Lord's satisfaction: she beautifies the Vrindavan forest with fragrant garlands and

melodious sounds, ensuring that the meeting place of Radha and Krishna embodies the perfect bucolic environment. Everything—including climate, flora, and fauna—must be just to Radha and Krishna's liking. Vrindadevi and her many maidservants set the stage for the divine couple's pleasure.

EIGHT NAMES

Because Tulasi is so dear to Krishna, Vaishnavas often chant her auspicious eight names: Vrindavani ("she who appears in the forest of Vrindavan"); Vrinda ("she who appears in the form of plants or trees"); Vishva-pujita ("she who is worshiped in every universe"); Pushpasara ("the greatest of all flowers"); Nandini ("she who brings faith and joy"); Krishna-jivani ("she who brings life to Lord Krishna"); Vishva-pavani ("she who purifies the entire universe"); and Tulasi ("she whose beauty is incomparable").

Notes

1. *Tulasi (Ocimum sanctum L.) belongs to the same family as the basil plant (Ocimum basilicum).*

"The Supreme God is one—Krishna—and the demigods are delegated with powers to manage this material world. These demigods are all living entities with different grades of material power. They cannot be equal to the Supreme God—Narayana, Vishnu, or Krishna."

—His Divine Grace A. C. Bhaktivedanta Swami Prabhupada

(*Bhagavad-gita As It Is* 4.12, purport)

The Demigods
Servants of Krishna

Much of the Hindu world recognizes 33 million gods (*devas*). Vaishnavas refer to them as demigods. The prefix "demi," from the Latin *dimidius,* or "half," indicates that these gods are "half-gods" and not the complete Personality of Godhead. In other words, they are not God but highly empowered beings who are subservient to God. Consequently, worship of the demigods is inappropriate; worship is reserved for the Supreme alone.

It is for this reason that Krishna says, "Those who are devotees of other gods (demigods) and worship them with faith actually worship only Me, O son of Kunti, but they do so without complete understanding." (*Bhagavad-gita* 9.25) The exact words Krishna uses are *avidhi-purvakam*—"in an inappropriate, unauthorized way." He further states, "Men in this world desire success in fruitive activities, and therefore they worship the demigods…." (*Bhagavad-gita* 4.12) In other words, demigod worship is materially motivated. Vaishnava commentators have asserted that material gain can never truly satisfy man, because he is a spiritual being. They further state that if one prays to demigods, one should do so for spiritual reasons. For instance, Ganesh, who is the remover of obstacles, can be asked to remove obstacles on the path to God realization. However, Vaishnava tradition stresses that even this is unnecessary, because all benedictions ultimately come from Krishna.

THE STATUS OF THE DEMIGODS ACCORDING TO BRAHMA-SAMHITA

To highlight Krishna's supremacy and to indicate the secondary status of the demigods, the demigod Brahma composed the treatise known as *Brahma-samhita*. The Gaudiya saint Bhaktisiddhanta Sarasvati Thakur has written in his commentary to this great work:

"The *Brahma-samhita* has refuted Panchopasana [Hinduism's traditional worship of five gods: Vishnu, Surya, Ganesh, Durga, and Shiva].... The worship of Vishnu as found in Panchopasana does not please Vishnu; it is heterodox and highly improper.... The worship of Vishnu as one of the five deities makes His highest dignity, which is without any equal, similar to that of the other deities, and [in that system] His Lordship is counted as one of several deities, which is a great spiritual offense.... It is the eternal duty of all *jivas* [living beings] to serve [only] Krishna, the Lord of all Lords. All other deities are His servitors. Their function is only to carry out Govinda's [Krishna's] commands. They will never acquire liberation who conceive of the deities as the different names and bodies of Vishnu instead of knowing them as His servitors. Five *shlokas* of the *Brahma-samhita* have described the natures of the five deities...: (1) "I (i.e., Brahma) adore the primeval Lord Govinda, in pursuance of whose order the Sun-god, the king of the planets and the eye of this world, performs his journey mounting the wheel of time." (2) "I adore the primeval Lord Govinda, whose lotus-like feet are always held by Ganesh on his head in order to obtain power for his function of destroying all the obstacles of the three worlds." (3) "I adore the primeval Lord Govinda, in accordance with whose will Durga, His external potency, conducts her function as the creating, preserving, and destroying agent of the world." (4) "I adore the primeval Lord Govinda, who transforms Himself as Shambhu [Shiva] for performing the work of destruction, just as milk is transformed into curd, which is neither the same as, nor different from, milk." (5) "I adore the primeval Lord Govinda, who manifests Himself as Vishnu in the same manner as one burning candle communicates its light to another candle which, though existing separately, is of the same quality as the first."[1]

Notes

1. Bhaktisiddhanta Sarasvati. 1934. "Shri Chaitanya's Teachings," 309–311. Madras: Shree Gaudiya Math.

SHIVA

Shiva, the ash-covered ascetic, the prince of the yogis, is one of the most widely worshiped deities in India. He wears a necklace of skulls and carries a snake in one hand and a trident in the other. With names such as Mahadeva ("the great god") and Nataraja ("the king of dancers"), Shiva ("the auspicious one") is venerated in ancient holy cities such as Benares, where his worshipers devote their lives to him. A verse from the scriptures explains Shiva's position in relation to divinity: "...[T]he Ganga is the greatest of all rivers, Lord Achyuta (Krishna) the best among deities, and Lord Shambhu (Shiva) the greatest Vaishnava...."

—*Shrimad Bhagavatam* 12.13.16

However, Shaivites (his worshipers) regard Shiva not just as the greatest devotee but as God Himself. There is a basis for this in scripture. As Lord Vishnu Himself explains in the *Bhagavatam* (4.7.50), "Brahma, Lord Shiva, and I are the supreme cause of the material manifestation. I am the Supersoul, the self-sufficient witness. But impersonally there is no difference between Brahma, Lord Shiva, and Me." In other words, all three divinities are one because they are all *avatars*, or descents of the Supreme for the purpose of creation, maintenance, and annihilation. In this context they are known as *guna-avatars* and preside over the modes of passion (embodied by Brahma, the creator), goodness (embodied by Vishnu, the maintainer), and ignorance (embodied by Shiva, the destroyer). All three personalities are considered various aspects of the same Godhead.

The *Mahabharata* (*Anushasana-parva* 135) also says that Vishnu and Shiva are nondifferent, and even counts the names Shiva, Sharva, Sthanu, Ishana, and Rudra—names traditionally identified with Shiva— among the thousand

names of Vishnu. Such identification between Shiva and the Supreme Lord, Vishnu, has led many to believe that all the gods mentioned in the Vedic literature are one. However, a close study of scripture reveals that while there is reason to see Shiva as not different from Vishnu, there is also reason to distinguish between them. According to the *Bhagavad-gita*, which is accepted by all classes of transcendentalists in India—including Vaishnavas and Shaivites—Vishnu (Krishna) is the Ultimate Godhead, before whom even Shiva must bow down. Krishna identifies Himself as the source of all material and spiritual worlds (10.8). Arjuna confirms that Krishna is supreme (10.12). Indeed Vishnu's (and thus Krishna's) supremacy is clearly defined as far back as the *Rig Veda*: "The lotus feet of Vishnu are the supreme objective of all the demigods. These lotus feet of the Lord are as enlightening as the sun in the sky." (*Rig Veda Samhita* 1.22.20)

Commenting on *Shrimad Bhagavatam* (3.9.16), Shrila Prabhupada says, "The Lord expands Himself into three—Vishnu, Brahma, and Shiva—for maintenance, creation, and destruction, respectively. Of the three principal agents controlling the three modes of material nature, Vishnu is the Almighty; even though He is within material nature for the purpose of maintenance, He is not controlled by the laws of material nature. The other two, Brahma and Shiva, although almost as greatly powerful as Vishnu, are within the control of the material energy of the Supreme Lord."

SHIVA LINGAM

An unusual iconic image through which Shiva is sometimes worshiped is made in the form of his genitalia (*lingam*). The ascetics known as Lingayats, also known as Vira-Shivas, are especially popular in South India. They wear miniature Shiva Lingas (phallic symbols) on their bodies. In this way they seek to remind themselves of their innate "Shiva nature," which, they feel, can be uncovered through vigorous austerity and yogic practices.

The origin of the Shiva Lingam is interesting. One day Parvati, Shiva's consort, took pity on a group of sages performing severe austerities in their forest dwelling. She asked Shiva to give them realization and release them from their penance. But Shiva refused, saying the sages were still prone to anger. To prove this he appeared in the forest as a handsome yogi and seduced the sages' wives. Incensed, the sages attacked Shiva and castrated him. But as soon as they did this Shiva disappeared and the entire cosmos began to shake. The sages, recognizing their impudence, begged Shiva to forgive them and calm the world. Shiva agreed on the condition that the sages, from that time forward, worship him in the form of his *lingam*.

Contemporary Shaivite worshipers usually fashion *lingams* from stone, marble, or metal. *Lingams* exist also in the form of sand and pebbles. Sometimes they are worshiped even in the form of anthills. The most revered *lingams* are those that are formed naturally, such as the Amarnath Lingam—an ice formation that never melts.

DURGA

Durga is the goddess of material creation. Whether she is called by her Greek name (Gaia), her African name (Oshun), her Egyptian name (Isis), or the hundreds of other names by which she is known throughout the world, the same divinity is being addressed. She is Mother Earth, known in Sanskrit as Bhu. The *Brahma-samhita* (5.43) explains that the material world is the venue for her service. The text describes four levels of existence.

The highest is Krishna's own abode, the most profound manifestation of the kingdom of God. Just below that is Hari-dham (Vaikuntha)—still the spiritual realm, but not quite as high as Krishna's abode. Still lower is Mahesh-dham, the dwelling place of Shiva and his devotees. Finally, there is Devi-dham, the material world, where the Goddess (the Mother of the universe) exerts control over the living entities residing there. Devi-dham consists of fourteen divisions of planetary systems. The *Brahma-samhita* (5.44) states the following about the Goddess: "The Lord's external potency, Maya, who is by nature a shadow of the *chit* [spiritual] potency, is worshiped by all people as Durga—the creating, preserving, and destroying agency of this mundane world. I adore the primeval Lord Govinda, in accordance with whose will Durga conducts herself."

In the verse just quoted, the presiding deity of Devi-dham is identified as Durga, a goddess whose physical appearance is both frightening and symbolic. She is often depicted with ten arms that represent ten kinds of fruitive activities. She rides on a ferocious lion signifying her heroism, and tramples Mahishasura—a buffalo demon that is said to represent all vices. Durga is the wife of Shiva. She has two sons, Karttikeya and Ganesh, who are the embodiments of beauty and success, respectively. In addition, she holds a snake that evokes destructive time, and holds twenty diverse weapons, each representing various pious activities enjoined in the Vedas for suppression of vices.

Durga incarnates in many forms. Although these manifestations, such as Kali and Uma, are worshiped as distinct deities with specific characteristics, they are nonetheless aspects of the same Goddess. In other words, when people in India speak of a generic "Goddess," they are usually referring to one of many overlapping feminine divinities: Durga, Kali, Mahadevi, Mayadevi (the queen of

the material energy), and so on. As Shiva's consort, Durga has various names: Parvati, Gauri, Uma, Devi, Bhavani, and so on. Her characteristics are diverse and manifest differently, depending on the aspect her devotee is focused on. Gauri, Uma, and Parvati are most benevolent and are generally portrayed as loving and kind. Durga is often represented as a heroic fighting goddess and can even be seen as bloodthirsty. However, she is not as blatantly bloodthirsty as her alter ego, Kali, who is the beneficiary of sacrificial animal offerings.

The Goddess is identified with *prakriti* (material nature) and *maya* (illusion). Indeed, two of her more popular names are Mulaprakriti ("the embodiment of primordial matter") and Mahamaya ("the great illusion"). This is significant. As Krishna says in the *Bhagavad-gita* (9.10): "The material energy [*prakriti*] is working under My direction, O son of Kunti, and is producing all moving and nonmoving beings." *Prakriti* is Durga. Krishna is in control by giving direction to Durga, His subordinate. When one doesn't acknowledge that, Durga becomes Mahamaya— the Great Illusion.

Durga in one of her more horrific forms.

MAYA

Mayadevi and her consort, Lord Shiva.

Simply stated, *maya* means "illusion." When extended, the term refers to "material existence." This is not to suggest, however, that all material existence is an illusion.

As Fritjof Capra writes in *The Tao of Physics* (Boston: Shambhala Publications, 1991, p. 88):

"Maya ... does not mean that the world is an illusion, as is often wrongly stated. The illusion merely lies in our point of view.... Maya is the illusion of [mistaking our relative perspective] for reality, of confusing the map with the territory."

Shrila Prabhupada defined *maya* as "that which is not," while his teacher, Shrila Bhaktisiddhanta Sarasvati Thakur, defined it as "that which is measurable." These two definitions appear contradictory. How can something be measurable if it does not exist?

The material world exists, but it is temporary. It exists like a dream—it has substance for some time, but eventually it fades. When Prabhupada refers to Maya as being "that which is not," he is referring to material existence, for it does not endure. It is "not," because it will soon fade into oblivion.

Bhaktisiddhanta Sarasvati's definition of *maya* also involves material existence: material things are measurable, while spiritual things are limitless. By definition, matter is temporary and limited (measurable), while spirit is eternal and unlimited (immeasurable). Thus, although Prabhupada and his teacher use different terminology and approach the subject from different angles, they define *maya* in much the same way: as being the very essence of material existence.

The demigoddess Maya (also called Kali or Durga) is the personification of this material existence. Shaktas (her worshipers) honor her as the supreme Goddess, the Mother of creation. It is interesting that the words "mother" (Sanskrit: *mata*) and "matter" are etymologically connected through

the same Latin root. Thus the terminology itself alludes to the identity between the Goddess and material nature.

"The goddess Durga," writes Prabhupada, "is the superintending deity of the material world, which is made of material elements. The demigods are simply different directors engaged in operating the departments of material activities, and they are under the influence of the same material energy, or Maya."

Durga, or Mayadevi, covers the living entities with her mystic potency, allowing them to live out their illusions in the material world. If, however, a living being chooses to return to spiritual consciousness, Mayadevi will manifest herself as Yogamaya, her spiritual counterpart. Yogamaya's purpose in the material world is just the opposite of Maya's. Whereas Maya creates a situation in which the living being lives an illusory existence in forgetfulness of God, Yogamaya creates an atmosphere whereby the living being can penetrate the world's illusions and relish intimacy with the source of all existence.

The awe-inspiring goddess is often depicted with many arms. She rides atop a ferocious animal while influencing inhabitants of the material world.

GANESH
THE ELEPHANT-HEADED DIVINITY

The elephant-headed deity Ganesh is revered by one billion Hindus worldwide. Viewed as the remover of obstacles and evil influences, Ganesh is often the guardian at thresholds and entrances. He is also worshiped just prior to religious ceremonies, both public and private, and is thus known as "the lord of beginnings."

Ganesh, with his human body, elephant head, and pot-belly, is perhaps the easiest of all demigods to identify. His images adorn the walls of temples, shops, and homes throughout India. He is pictured in standing, sitting, or dancing poses, with his jolly elephant face looking straight ahead. As Vyasadeva's scribe, Ganesh wrote down a portion of the Vedic literature that Vyasa dictated to him verse by verse. Thus he is at times depicted with quill on palm leaf. He is missing one tusk, a piece of which can sometimes be seen in one of his four hands. In another hand he holds a hatchet (*parashu*) which, according to some texts, is for "cutting away illusion and false teachings." Another of Ganesh's hands is gesturing fearlessness and reassurance (*varada-hasta-mudra*). He also holds a goad (*ankusha*), like the one used by an elephant trainer. The goad symbolizes Ganesh's insistence on proper training (*sadhana*) and spiritual discipline. In another hand Ganesh often holds a noose (*pasha*) used for restraining wild animals, and here representing the restraint of passion and the desires born of lust. Sometimes Ganesh is seen holding sweets (*modaka*) as well, for it is said that he has an inordinate fondness for them. Hence the belly.

Vedic texts describe Ganesh as the son of Shiva and Parvati (Durga), although his sonship is peculiar. According to one version, Shiva "emits" a son from his own body. The child is handsome, with alluring features, and grows up to be a seducer of women. Parvati is offended by her son's exploits and curses him to have the head of an elephant and a big belly—in other words, to be unattractive. He gradually settles down, however, with two wives: Buddhi ("wisdom") and Siddhi ("success"), who can see beyond his physical ugliness. As time passes, Ganesh becomes the commander (*gana-isha* or *gana-pati*) of Shiva's troops. Because he becomes well known as one who removes obstacles for the demigods or the devotees and one who creates obstacles for the demons, he is called Vinayaka ("one who removes [obstacles]") and Vighneshvara ("lord of obstacles").

In another, more popular version of the Ganesh story, Parvati wants to feel protected from her passionate husband Shiva, especially while bathing. From her own perspiration she creates a son and appoints him to be the guardian of her quarters. Soon Shiva seeks admission into Parvati's inner chambers. Unaware of Shiva's identity, Ganesh refuses him entrance and pushes him away from Parvati's door. The enraged Shiva, not one to be slighted in any way, summons his attendants (*ganas*) to do away with this overly assertive attendant. But Ganesh defeats them one by one. Finally, Vishnu arrives and, drawing upon His *shakti* (mystic potency), creates confusion on all sides, thus enabling Shiva to cut off Ganesh's head. Parvati is furious at what has become of her "son." She decides to send a multitude of goddesses to harass the demigods. The women thus make clear to the noble gods that their queen can be appeased only if her guardian is totally resuscitated. Shiva tells the gods to go north and to cut off the head of the first living being that they see; this head would then be mystically placed on the body of the recently decapitated Ganesh, who would then come back to external consciousness. As fate would have it, the first living being to cross the path of the gods is an elephant.

All religions contain elements that extend the boundaries of reason. As J. Stillson Judah, a scholar associated with the Graduate Theological Union at the University of California and author of the first major academic study on the Hare Krishna movement, points out:

"If to the outsider the 'pastimes of Krishna' [or that of Lord Ganesh] appear miraculous and illogical, the following question must be asked. Does not the awareness of a higher reality, which all religions declare to be a divine mystery, come most often through participation in the irrational, the paradox—and, for the disbeliever, the absurd? For many Buddhists, it may emerge through meditating on the paradoxes of the 'pragya-paramita' or the nonsensical 'ko-ans'; for the Pentecostals, it speaks through the incoherent babble of glossolalia; for the Roman Catholics, it involves the mystery of the transubstantiation of the bread and wine into the body and blood of Christ during the Mass; for the Moslem, it may occur during the pilgrimage to Mecca, when he trots between the hills of Saffa and Marwah imitating Hagar's search for water."

If the story of Ganesh seems fantastic and unbelievable, let us ask ourselves why. Ganesh wouldn't have it any other way!

BRAHMA
THE FIRST CREATED BEING

According to the Puranas, the material cosmos begins with Brahma, a multiheaded demigod from the highest planet (Brahmaloka) in the cosmos. He is known as Pitamaha, the Grandfather, as he is the first created being as well as the original instructor (guru) of the sages.

Vaishnavas consider Brahma to be the Lord's manifestation (*guna-avatar*) who presides over the mode of passion. Brahma's passionate nature is put to work, and he is engaged in creation. Thus he is the creator god and the progenitor of mankind, as distinct from Vishnu, who is seen as the preserver (and master of the mode of goodness), and Shiva, the destroyer (who presides over the mode of ignorance). In popular Hinduism, this triad of *avatars* (*trimurti*) is viewed as merely diverse forms of one and the same God. However, a careful study reveals that Shiva and Brahma (demigods) are subservient to Vishnu (or Krishna, the Supreme Godhead).

Brahma's enlightenment is described in the *Shrimad Bhagavatam* (2.9). At the dawn of creation, he takes birth on a lotus that sprouts from the divine navel of Vishnu.

Finding himself in a new world, Brahma is ignorant of both his own identity and the purpose of life. In an attempt to understand his origin, he climbs down the stem of the spiritual lotus, but finds no answer to his dilemma. Finally, he hears the voice of his Lord and Master, Vishnu, calling out two syllables: *"ta-pa"* (literally "austerity" or "penance"). These syllables are pregnant with meaning, and Brahma obeys by performing austerity in the form of meditation for one thousand celestial years (billions of earth years). At the end of this period, Brahma is able to see the Lord's abode and then the Supreme Lord Himself. The Supreme recites for him the four seminal verses of the *Shrimad Bhagavatam*— verses which formulate the meaning of life. The purification that comes from hearing the Lord's voice allows Brahma to create the material universe.

In his *Brahma-samhita* (5.24–29), Lord Brahma adds details to the *Bhagavatam* version of the story of his enlightenment. According to Brahma, at the beginning of time he is engulfed in total darkness and is bewildered about his service as creator of the universe. At that time, Sarasvati, the divine consort of the Supreme Lord, appears before Brahma. She instructs him to meditate upon the confidential *Kama-bija-mantra*, promising that by its recitation he will receive all that he needs. After meditating on this mantra for one hundred celestial years, Brahma hears the sound of Krishna's flute. He tries to reproduce the sound with his own lips, but instead finds that he is uttering the esoteric *Kama-gayatri-mantra*. This mantra purifies him of all illusion, and he is able to proceed with his service of creating the material universes on Krishna's behalf.

Brahma begins each day by meditating on the Supreme Lord. He prays that he may "engage in the Lord's service in the creation of the material world," and that he may not be materially affected by his works, for thus he "may be able to give up the false prestige of being the creator." (*Shrimad Bhagavatam* 3.9.23) In other words, Brahma admits his dependence on the Lord. Thus, unlike many other demigods, Brahma is rarely mistaken for the Supreme.

SARASVATI
GODDESS OF LEARNING

Sarasvati is glorified in the oldest portions of the Vedic literature as wisdom personified. Her fame has spread to the Buddhist tradition, where she is depicted as the consort of Manjushri, the god of wisdom. The great Vaishnava text *Shrimad Bhagavatam* (1.2.4) proclaims that her name should be evoked before any recital of this seminal scripture. Clearly, then, her position is special and is another indication of the accord given to the feminine in the Vaishnava tradition.

The Puranas tell us that Sarasvati incarnated both as Brahma's wife and as the sacred Sarasvati River. When Brahma, the primeval created being, was bewildered about how to create the material universe, it was Mother Sarasvati who came to his aid (*Brahma-samhita* 5.24–25). Giving him the Gayatri-mantra, she told him that by meditating on it all his desires would be fulfilled. He followed her advice, as mentioned earlier, and the material cosmos was born.

Sarasvati is depicted as clad in elegant white or red robes, sitting on a white lotus. In her hands she carries a book (to symbolize learning), *japa* beads (which, like the rosary in the West, are used to keep track of one's chanting), and a vina (a stringed instrument used in traditional Indian music). In the *Rig Veda*, Sarasvati is related to the

THE SARASVATI RIVER

The famous Sarasvati River flows through North India and, according to the *Mahabharata* (*Adi-parva* 16.19), anyone who drinks her waters will become free from sin. Unfortunately, the river is not so easy to locate. Although thousands of years ago, during the time of the *Rig Veda*, people knew her exact location, today the river is invisible to mortal eyes. Unlike the Yamuna or the Ganges, the Sarasvati cannot be found by scouting North Indian holy rivers. Still, it is said that great yogis can see her if they go to the confluence of the three rivers at modern Allahabad.

Geological evidence suggests that the Sarasvati (known to geologists as the Ghaggar-Hakra River) dried out around 1900 B.C.E. However, aerial infrared scanning reveals the course of the ancient river even today. Using these methods, geographers locate the mouth of the original Sarasvati near the Rann of Kutch, adjacent to the Thar Desert. Thus pilgrims can go and see where the holy river once quenched the thirst of self-realized souls.

Goddess of Sound (Vak) and is often identified not only as the goddess of learning but of music as well. Her mount is generally a swan, but sometimes a ram, an owl, a parrot, a lotus, or a peacock. She is the very essence of knowledge; beautiful thoughts, mellifluously articulated, originate by her grace.

Hanuman

Monkeys are a common sight in many parts of India. The langur—a large simian of slender build with pale gray fur, long tail, and black face, hands, and feet—can be found in the woods as well as at ruins and sacred sites. It is said that these monkeys are modern-day descendants of Hanuman, the great monkey-hero, servant of Rama.

anuman is among the most popular sacred figures in India. He is often portrayed kneeling with reverentially joined palms before his Lord, Ramachandra, Sita (Rama's wife), and Lakshman (Rama's brother).

Hanuman first appears in the fourth book of Valmiki's *Ramayana* (*Kishkindha-khanda*), but he does not occupy center stage until the fifth book (*Sundara-khanda*). It is only here that we learn of his exemplary devotion to Sita and Rama. In fact, Hanuman is sometimes described as tearing open his chest to reveal Rama's image in his heart. He is also depicted soaring through the sky with a Himalayan peak in his hand. At other times, his hands are in the gesture (*mudra*) for removing fear (*abhaya*) and giving benedictions (*varada*).

In the final book of the *Ramayana* (*Uttara-khanda*), the sage Valmiki tells of Hanuman's birth and childhood. As a young child, Hanuman once mistook the sun for a fruit. When he tried to capture the sun, the demigod Indra knocked him down and broke his jaw with a thunderbolt. Hanuman's compassionate father, the wind-god, then induced other gods to shower Hanuman with extraordinary boons. This accounts for Hanuman's well-known physical prowess and supernatural abilities. In youth, Hanuman playfully vandalized the ashrams of forest ascetics, who reacted by cursing him to forget his powers until he would meet Lord Rama. Hanuman would then come into his own and use his powers for the ultimate good of all.

Hanuman was indeed a monkey. Valmiki describes him by using the word *vanara*, originally meaning "proper to the forest," "forest animal," although it soon came to refer specifically to monkeys. Hanuman often displayed the qualities typical of

Hanuman devotee as the monkey-hero in a Ramayana performance.

THE HIDDEN GLORY OF INDIA

Hanuman approaches Sita on Rama's behalf.

his descendants. As cited in the *Ramayana* (5.53.111), he had a tendency to jump from tree to tree and was a general mischief-maker.

Yet Hanuman and his monkey brethren were more like human beings. Valmiki makes this clear when he writes about their speech, clothing, funerals, dwelling places, and consecration festivals. In other words, Hanuman and the *vanaras* of Treta-yuga (hundreds of thousands of years ago) were half-monkey, half-human. But they were unmistakably empowered semi-divine beings as well. Having all mystic yogic perfections in full, they could take on any form or become large or small. Valmiki writes that Hanuman could leap into the air like a magical being. Yet his greatest power, says Valmiki, was his devotion to Rama.

HANUMAN: GOD OR DEVOTEE?

Great literary and poetic works, such as the *Hanuman Chalisa*, appeared in Medieval India, elevating Hanuman to the status of a god. Impressed by Hanuman's amazing qualities, many people in India see him as a divinity on his own, independent of Rama. The scriptures, however, make it clear that Hanuman and the *vanaras* are devotees, not gods. Throughout the *Sundara-khanda*, the *Ramayana* clearly shows Rama's superior status. There, in beautiful soliloquies suffused with devotion, Hanuman repeatedly showers Rama with praise. Thus Hanuman is clearly the *bhakta*, the devotee, and Rama the Bhagavan, the Lord.

Hanuman flees from the wrathful Ravana.

"Time I am, the great destroyer of the worlds..."
—Lord Krishna
Bhagavad-gita 11.32

THE four ages

In contrast to the Western concept of linear time, the sacred texts of India view reality from the perspective of cycles called yugas. Our current cycle of history is seen as one of many stages that recur eternally. Ages turn into new ages, and then back again. Nature shows hints of this throughout life: the seasons repeat themselves, the days of the week recur, day turns into night and then day again.

Indian seers take this as an indicator of what happens in all aspects of reality: life does not end with death; rather, the soul is reborn in a new body. In this way, the soul lives through a cycle of lives, much as the various ages associated with cosmic time repeat themselves.

History moves in a succession of great cycles called *divya-yugas*. The Vedic texts give minute details on the length of these cycles. Each *divya-yuga* is composed of four ages progressively declining in length: Satya-yuga (or sometimes Krita-yuga), which lasts 1,728,000 years; Treta-yuga, which lasts 1,296,000 years; Dvapara-yuga, which lasts 864,000 years; and Kali-yuga, our current age, which lasts 432,000 years. These four periods are called the golden, silver, copper, and iron ages, respectively.

We are now more than 5,000 years into Kali-yuga. After that, in roughly 427,000 years, there will be a partial destruction of the universe, and then a new Satya-yuga will dawn.[1] According to the texts, as the ages decline in length from Satya- to Kali-yuga, piety and other virtues also diminish in a commensurate way.

The four *yugas* altogether (and thus one *divya-yuga*) last 4,320,000 human years. One thousand such cycles (4.32 billion years) make up merely one day in the life of Brahma. Each day is followed by a night of equal length. During the night, Brahma sleeps and most planets are submerged in waters of devastation. At the end of the night, Brahma awakens and another day of one thousand cycles commences. Three hundred and sixty of these days and nights make up one of Brahma's years; Brahma lives one hundred such years.

Notes

1. Regarding methods of worship in each of the ages: In Satya-yuga one attained the Absolute through deep meditation; in Treta-yuga, through opulent sacrifices; in Dvapara-yuga, through Deity (iconic) worship; and in Kali, through chanting the holy name of the Lord.

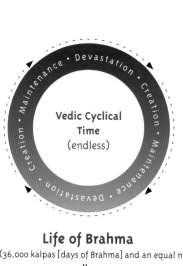

Lord Brahma lives for the duration of the universe, which is repeatedly created and destroyed. Every time the universe is created, a new Brahma is born. Both full and partial devastations of the universe occur at regular intervals. Brahma's present day began 2.3 billion years ago.

Life of Brahma

311.04 trillion years (36,000 kalpas [days of Brahma] and an equal number of nights)

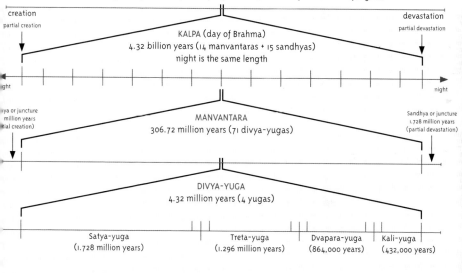

creation   devastation

partial creation   partial devastation

KALPA (day of Brahma)
4.32 billion years (14 manvantaras + 15 sandhyas)
night is the same length

ght   night

...dhya or juncture
...million years
...tial creation)

Sandhya or juncture
1.728 million years
(partial devastation)

MANVANTARA
306.72 million years (71 divya-yugas)

DIVYA-YUGA
4.32 million years (4 yugas)

| Satya-yuga
(1.728 million years) | Treta-yuga
(1.296 million years) | Dvapara-yuga
(864,000 years) | Kali-yuga
(432,000 years) |

Judeo-Christian/Modern Scientific
(Linear Time—begins & ends)

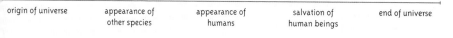

origin of universe   appearance of
other species   appearance of
humans   salvation of
human beings   end of universe

Time

A discussion of the broad concept of time found in the Vaishnava tradition naturally begins with a description of the four yugas. However, the Vaishnava concept of time goes far beyond the basic yuga cycle. The solar calendar divides the year into six seasons (determined astronomically): *vasanta* (spring), *grishma* (hot season), *varsha* (rainy season), *sharad* (autumn), *hemanta* (winter), and *shishira* (cool season). Further, the 24-hour solar day is divided into 30 *muhurtas* (48 minutes each). A *muhurta* is again divided into 2 *ghatis* (of 24 minutes each). Each *ghati* is broken down into 30 *kalas* (of 48 seconds each). Each *kala* is divided into 2 *palas* (of 24 seconds each), and each *pala* into 6 *pranas* (of 4 seconds each). Each *prana* is divided into 10 *vipalas* (of 0.4 seconds each), and each *vipala* into 60 *prativipalas* (0.00666 seconds each). In this way, time is calculated down to the most minute measurements.

Theologically, the Vedic literature discusses time as a potency of God. It is measured in terms of the movements of atomic particles and is identified with Krisna Himself, or with His all-pervading impersonal aspect. This atomic particle (called *anu*) is among the fundamental building blocks of material nature. The *Bhagavatam* elaborates, explaining how atoms take up material space and are consequently subject to time (since time is measured in terms of motion in space). Because both space and time are material, the *Bhagavatam* connects them to *maya*, the illusion. In other words, all changes that result from the vicissitudes of time

are temporary, like a dream. Only Krishna and His *avatars*, belonging to the spiritual domain, are beyond the dictates of time.

However, in some ways time does appear to exist in the spiritual realm. Krishna, in His pastimes, rises in the morning, milks the cows, then eats breakfast, goes to the forest with His friends and the cows, plays all day, and in the evening returns to Vrindavan village, etc. It must be noted, though, that all these pastimes exist simultaneously. Each moment is eternally present. Since this constitutes an unfathomable concept of time, the Vedic literature concludes that, in the spiritual realm, time (as we know it) is conspicuous by its absence.

Although the spiritual world is free from time as we know it, all beings in the material world are subject to time and thus must suffer repeated birth and death. They appear in the world, and gradually go through six phases of life: birth, growth, persistence (staying for some time), production of by-products, dwindling, and, finally, death.

VEDIC COSMOLOGY

Cosmology refers to the study of the physical universe, including its meaning and structure. One might wonder, therefore, why Vaishnava texts, which focus on the soul and its relation to God, have anything to say about this subject. The external universe, after all, is clearly a material phenomenon as opposed to a spiritual one. And yet one who understands Vaishnavism knows that it is concerned not just with spiritual subjects as such but also with the spiritual dimension of all things material. Vaishnavas are thus keen to understand and use this universe and its accoutrements in the service of the Divine. In this spirit, the Vedic literature contains detailed analyses of the material universes and how living in one or another planetary system might be advantageous or disadvantageous in one's pursuit of God.

Amazingly, these ancient texts offer details of the universe still unknown in modern studies of the subject. One may accept or reject this information, but its sheer volume makes one wonder: Where did the ancients get these elaborate details, and why does their knowledge of cosmology seem so consistent and thorough?

The most important texts on Vedic cosmology may well be the *Bhagavatam* and the *Vishnu Purana*, but the subject is explained in all its complexity in the *Surya-siddhanta*, a mystical text revealed by a demigod from the sun almost two million years ago. Basically, the cosmology found therein divides material existence into innumerable universes, each one contained within a spherical shell composed of layers of elemental matter. Each universe contains fourteen planetary systems, from higher to lower. Interestingly, Vedic cosmology is geocentric, locating the Earth and similar planets midway on the axis of these planetary systems. It is not, however, ethnocentric, for Mount Meru, recognized in this system as the center of the universe, is found far from the Indian subcontinent. It should be noted, though, that in a

mystical sense Vrindavan is considered the center of the universe.

Since earthly planets are considered equidistant from both extremes of the cosmos, the earthly realm is considered an ideal middle ground for working out one's karma, between the heavenly delights of the upper spheres and the torturous pain of the lower planets. Great demigods from the higher dimensions thus pray for birth on earth, for here they can avoid sensuality long enough to engage in the service of the Lord; tormented beings from the lower planets also hope for birth in the earthly region, for here they can avoid pain long enough to pursue higher goals.

The seven netherworlds are each named in the Vedic texts, and what the unfortunates who live there undergo is described in graphic detail. The earthly middle is made up of Svarloka, Bhuvarloka, and Bhurloka (Earth). From here one may graduate to the four higher planetary systems, known as Maharloka, Janaloka, Tapoloka, and Satyaloka, the highest planets of the demigods—if one acts piously and accrues good karma. Otherwise, one falls back down to the lower planets.

Vedic texts describe the prodigious duration of life and day-to-day interests of beings on the upper planets, sparing no details. Again, it is astounding that these ancient texts present such extremely detailed knowledge about a subject that would appear to be beyond its scope. For more on this subject, see *Mysteries of the Sacred Universe*, by Richard L. Thompson (Alachua, Florida: Govardhana Hill Publishing, 1999).

A Passage to Matter

Vedic texts describe that when one first incarnates in the material world, one may be born as Brahma, a primary being in one of the highest material planets. Because the soul's Brahma incarnation is initially pure, having no experience of the material world, its body is not grossly material. Rather, it is comprised of subtle matter only—it is made of pure intelligence. But then, due to association with the irrational passions borne of having a nonspiritual body, one falls to the lowest species, known as the Indragopa, a single-celled organism on a lower planet. From there, one gradually evolves through the 8,400,000 species of life, and eventually takes birth on an earthly planet. From here, again, one can go up, or go down.

THE
SPIRITUAL
SKY

While in the previous pages we have briefly explained the fourteen divisions of material planetary systems, here we will explore the polydimensional universe known as the Spiritual Sky. Though the material cosmos is inconceivably vast, in comparison to the world of the spirit, it seems like little more than a small cardboard box.

Vaishnava texts describe Devi-dham, or the material world, as the lowest of all possible realms. Mahesh-dham, or the abode of Lord Shiva, is slightly higher than the multifarious universes that make up Devi-dham. The worlds encompassed by both Devi-dham and Mahesh-dham range from the grossly material, such as those in the lower and middle planetary systems (like Earth), up to those that are composed almost exclusively of subtle energy, such as mind, intelligence, and ego.

Beyond these lesser realms is Hari-dham, also known as Vaikuntha. This is the Spiritual Sky proper, where there are no material imperfections and life is eternal. And above the highest realm in Hari-dham is Goloka, Krishna's supreme abode. Details on why Goloka is the topmost spiritual abode can be found in both the *Brahma-samhita* and the writings of the Six Goswamis of Vrindavan.

To elaborate, on the outer shell of the material cosmos is the Viraja River, beyond which one finds the freed souls, or those liberated from material existence. Further still is the Paravyoma, where infinite numbers of *avatars*, or partial manifestations of Krishna, reside. Here one can locate the planets of Narasimha, Vamana, and Rama, for example, and devotees of these particular manifestations of Godhead may go to these spiritual realms after death. Above all other realms is Krishna's supreme planet, Goloka, which can manifest as Dvaraka, where opulence reigns supreme; as Mathura, where opulence is mixed with sweetness; and, ultimately, as Vrindavan, where all lordly power is eclipsed by love.

Expansions of these three latter abodes exist on Earth, and their material counterparts are considered nondifferent from their corresponding spiritual regions.

KARMA & REINCARNATION

All beings are born and, in time, all die. According to the Vaishnava tradition, all beings are then born again. The idea of reincarnation—the cyclical round of births and deaths that are experienced but not remembered—and the closely related concept of karma ("for every action there is a corresponding reaction") have been an integral part of Indian culture since time immemorial. Indeed, one of the most ancient Indic texts, the *Shatapatha Brahmana* (10.4.3.1), states, "Whoever knows Truth conquers recurring death and attains a full life." The exact words—*punar mrityu* ("recurring death")—traditionally refer to reincarnation, for, according to the original Sanskrit, they indicate being born, dying, and being born again (only to die again). The Vaishnava understanding of reincarnation and its related concepts can be summarized in the following three principles:

1. Each living entity is a soul within a material body. Vedic texts are precise regarding the soul within the body: "When the upper point of a hair is divided into one hundred parts, and each part is further divided into one hundred parts, each such part is the dimension of the spirit soul." (*Shvetashvatara Upanishad* 5.9) Accordingly, the tradition teaches that the universe contains innumerable particles of spiritual atoms—souls—measured as one ten-thousandth of the upper portion of a hair. Knowledge of the soul's dimensions is augmented by information regarding the position of the soul in the body: "The soul is atomic in size and can be perceived by perfect intelligence. This atomic soul is floating in the five kinds of air (*prana, apana, vyana, samana,* and *udana*). It is situated within the heart and spreads its influence all over the body of the embodied living entities. When the soul is purified from the contamination of the five kinds of

material air, its spiritual influence is exhibited." (*Mundaka Upanishad* 3.1.9) The soul is thus caught in the body, and from the moment of its birth falsely identifies with the body.

In one lifetime an individual passes through many different bodies—baby, child, youth, adult, and so on—but remains the same person. The soul does not change; what changes is the body. The *Bhagavad-gita* (2.13) states: "As the embodied soul continuously passes, in this body, from boyhood to youth to old age, so at death the same soul passes into another body."

2. Actions performed in this body determine the next body. Vaishnava texts assert that the soul's transmigration from body to body does not take place in a random way. The soul's journey is instigated by subtle desires and charted according to karma, or prior actions, whether earlier in this life or in previous existences. It is for this reason that the various species are created—each type of body is equipped with a particular sensual forte. Individuals inhabit bodies according to their tastes and desires. For example, for a human being inclined to sluggishness and sleep, the body of a bear (who sleeps for months at a time) may be more appropriate.

3. The soul can escape rebirth by developing consciousness of God. Krishna says in the *Bhagavad-gita* (8.15), "After attaining Me, the great souls, who are yogis in devotion, are never born again...." Thus, the Vaishnava tradition teaches that the process of *bhakti-yoga* (devotional

yoga) can free one from the cycle of birth and death. As stated in the *Brahma-samhita* (5.59), "The highest devotion is attained by constant endeavor for self-realization with the help of scriptural evidence, theistic conduct, and perseverance in practice."

A. L. Herman, professor of philosophy at the University of Wisconsin–Stevens Point, explains the importance of *bhakti-yoga* in the following manner:

"Bhakti-yoga, 'the Way of Adoration,' offers a way out of the problem of [reincarnation] by showing the path of selfless devotion to God. In other words, Bhakti-yoga...produces actions without karmic residues as the Bhakta [devotee] dedicates his actions and their consequences to an adored God; as a result, the karma generated by the act becomes God's and not the bhakta's. The conclusion is that the problem of suffering is solved once again, as the cause of duhkha, desire, is crushed in the surrendering to God of all the fruits of one's labors. And, once again, the way to heaven is open."[1]

Krishna states, "From the highest planet in the material world down to the lowest, all are places of misery, wherein repeated birth and death take place. But one who attains to My abode never takes birth again." (*Bhagavad-gita* 8.16)

Notes

1. A. L. Herman. 1991. *A Brief Introduction to Hinduism*, 119. San Francisco: Westview Press.

THE VICTOR OF MY HEART

Hail Thee, O Chaitanya—the victor of my heart. Mark the rhythm of this mystic dance, in lofty ecstasy quite alone. Merrily sounds the tabor, and the cymbals' notes keep time.

The joyous band following him sing and dance merrily, merrily.

He steps a pace or two onwards, in his dancing gait, and knows no rest. For he is intoxicated with his own over-flowing joy.

O my heart's Lord, how can I express the love I have for Thee?

Shah Akbar craves a drop from the sea of Thy love and piety.

—Verses by Akbar
quoted in D.C. Sen. 1922. Chaitanya and His Age. Calcutta: University of Calcutta Press.

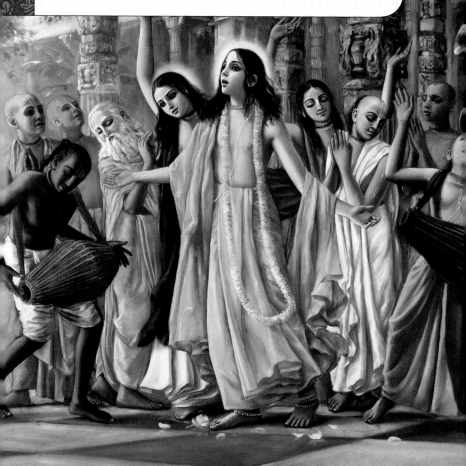

SHRI CHAITANYA

AN INTRODUCTION

Shri Chaitanya Mahaprabhu (1486–1533) is considered a combined manifestation of **Radha** and **Krishna**. This esoteric incarnation of God brought to the world a process of spirituality by which one can enter into the deepest realms of transcendence.

In the *Shrimad Bhagavatam* (7.9.38) God is called "Tri-yuga"—"He who appears in only three of the four ages (Satya, Treta, Dvapara, and Kali)." This is so because in the fourth age (Kali) He manifests as the Channa ("secret") Avatar, or the special, hidden incarnation. His existence in Kali-yuga is considered hidden because, unlike other *avatars*, Channa Avatar does not reveal Himself as an incarnation. Rather, He displays His pastimes in the guise of His own devotee, allowing only His most intimate followers to know of His divinity. Still, those who study the scriptures will know who He is.

The Puranas explain that in Satya-yuga the Lord comes in a white color; in Treta, reddish; in Dvapara, blackish; and in Kali, golden. Shri Chaitanya is distinguished by His golden color, as has been noted by all His biographers.

Vedic and post-Vedic writings describe *avatars* in considerable detail: their "parentage," the town where they appear, the mission they seek to accomplish, and various specifics of this nature. Direct, corroborative statements about the divinity of Shri Chaitanya are found in the *Mahabharata* and *Shrimad Bhagavatam*, compiled centuries before Shri Chaitanya's birth. An entire text that is considered part of the *Atharva Veda* and is known as the *Chaitanya Upanishad* foretells His glories. The *Krishna-yamala* and *Brahma-yamala* specifically mention His mother's name and the town of His birth, Navadvip. These two scriptures also relate His mission: propagating the Sankirtan movement, which focuses on the congregational chanting of the holy name of God.

The *Vayu Purana* says: "In the Age of Kali, when the Sankirtan movement is inaugurated, Krishna will descend as the divine son of Sachidevi." The *Bhagavatam* substantiates the statement about Shri Chaitanya Mahaprabhu being the "golden" *avatar* of Kali-yuga, and adds further information about the Sankirtan movement: "In the Age of Kali the incarnation of the Lord always chants the holy name 'Krishna' in the company of His associates. His complexion is not blackish but golden. The wise worship Him by chanting His name in congregation." (*Shrimad Bhagavatam* 11.5.32) Indeed, Shri Chaitanya and His teachings of divine love through congregational chanting of the holy name are the hidden glory of India—India's actual glory.

SHRI CHAITANYA
HIS LIFE

"I could believe only in a God who understood how to dance." — Friedrich Nietzsche

Chaitanya Mahaprabhu was born on February 18, 1486. His birth name was Vishvambhar Mishra, but later He became popular as Nimai Pandit, and still later, after becoming a renunciant, as Chaitanya Mahaprabhu. He was born in the holy town of Navadvip, also known as Mayapur, in West Bengal.

Mahaprabhu's parents— Jagan-nath Mishra and Sachidevi— had suffered through the deaths of their first eight children, all girls. The birth of Vishvarup, Mahaprabhu's elder brother, signaled a change in their lives. Soon after, Mahaprabhu was born.

When Mahaprabhu was about eight years of age, He began school under the tutelage of Gangadas Pandit. Two years later, in 1496, He became known as a great scholar, having mastered logic, hermeneutics, philosophy, and several languages. It was in this year, too, that His elder brother, Vishvarup, took *sannyas*, the renounced order of life, and became a traveling mendicant. This event had a deep influence on young Mahaprabhu.

Four years later, in the year 1500,

He married Lakshmipriya, and when she passed away untimely, He remarried. Vishnupriya, greatly respected in the Vaishnava community, became His second wife.

In 1503 Shri Chaitanya Mahaprabhu traveled to Gaya, in Bihar province, to perform the funeral rites for His father. While in Gaya, He met Ishvara Puri, a great saint, and took initiation from him. It is said that immediately after initiation, by chanting the mantras His teacher gave Him, Mahaprabhu became God-intoxicated. According to sacred texts, spiritual sound virtually comes to life when it is bestowed upon

a disciple by a genuine spiritual teacher. The chanter thus associates with God through His holy name in the form of a mantra and experiences spiritual bliss culminating in love of God.

Apropos of this, Shri Chaitanya was enraptured by the holy name of Krishna. He was totally given to theomania, which made Him chant and dance in ecstasy. His biographers recount that He spontaneously danced with wild abandon, His followers joining Him in His vigorous chanting episodes. After His initiation Shri Chaitanya also performed many miracles—curing lepers, bringing the dead back to life, appearing in several places at once, manifesting divine forms, etc. These many supernatural occurrences were documented by His contemporaries. Accomplished devotional practitioners recognized Shri Chaitanya in His own time, as Jesus was earlier recognized by his disciples.

In the beginning of 1510, when Chaitanya Mahaprabhu was twenty-four, He traveled to nearby Katwa and was initiated there into the renounced order of life (*sannyas*). The initiation was performed by Keshava Bharati, a renowned monk of the impersonalistic school, who was soon to be converted by Mahaprabhu Himself. After His *sannyas* initiation, Mahaprabhu went to Vrindavan and then to Puri, gradually undertaking a two-year tour of South India. During these travels He met many notable personalities, including the Six Goswamis of Vrindavan and Ramananda Roy, to whom He revealed His divine essence as Radha and Krishna combined.

After inundating the subcontinent with His message of divine love, Chaitanya Mahaprabhu returned to Jagannath Puri. As He passed His days among His associates, He was more and more overtaken by *radha-bhava*, the ecstasy associated with Radharani's love for Krishna. In the last few years of His manifest life, Mahaprabhu even exhibited complete contraction of His bodily limbs. This is called *dvadashadasha* and occurs only in the twelfth stage of *mahabhava*, one of the most exalted levels of devotional mysticism. Such stages of devotion are very rarely achieved. Chaitanya Mahaprabhu lived out His final days sharing His secret of divine love with His most intimate associates.

Shri Chaitanya dances in ecstasy before the Ratha-yatra carts.

SHRI CHAITANYA

HIS TEACHINGS

Shri Chaitanya composed eight Sanskrit prayers known as the **Shikshashtakam**. Gaudiya Vaishnavas see them as the **essence** of all **devotional moods** and spiritual instructions.

The first of the eight prayers espouses the glory of chanting the holy name of Krishna:

"Let there be all victory for the chanting of Krishna's holy name, which can cleanse the mirror of the heart and stop the miseries of the blazing fire of material existence. That chanting is the waxing moon that spreads the lotus of good fortune for all living entities. It is the life and soul of all education. The chanting of the holy name of Krishna expands the blissful ocean of transcendental life. It gives a cooling effect to everyone, and enables one to taste full nectar at every step."

In the second verse, in the mood of a sincere devotee, Mahaprabhu expounds the potency of the holy name and the misfortune of not having the desire to chant: "My Lord, O Supreme Personality of Godhead, in Your holy name there is all good fortune for the living entity, and therefore You have many names, such as Krishna and Govinda,

by which You expand Yourself. These names are invested with all Your potencies, and there are no hard and fast rules for chanting them. My dear Lord, although You bestow such mercy on the fallen, conditioned souls by liberally teaching Your holy names, I am so unfortunate that I commit offenses while chanting these names, and therefore I do not achieve attachment for chanting."

The third verse describes the humble person who is eligible to chant the Lord's name purely: "One who thinks himself lower than the grass, who is more tolerant than a tree, and who does not expect personal honor but is instead always ready to give all respect to others, can easily chant the holy name of the Lord all the time."

The fourth verse establishes the exclusivity of purpose necessary for pure chanting: "O Lord of the universe, I do not desire material wealth, followers, a beautiful wife, or fruitive activities described in

Shri Chaitanya with His associates.

flowery language. All I want, life after life, is pure, unmotivated devotional service unto You."

In the fifth verse, Shri Chaitanya cites the reason for material conditioning and speaks of the humility required to become free: "O my Lord, O Krishna, son of Maharaj Nanda, I am Your eternal servant, but because of my fruitive acts I have fallen into this horrible ocean of nescience. Please be causelessly merciful to me. Consider me a particle of dust at Your lotus feet."

In the sixth verse, a hint is given of the three external symptoms that accompany the dawn of true love for God: "My dear Lord, when will my eyes be beautified by tears that constantly glide down as I chant Your holy name? When will my voice falter and all of the hairs of my body stand on end in transcendental happiness as I chant Your name?"

The seventh verse describes the soul who is nearing perfection. In a mood of inconceivably blissful separation, the pure devotee becomes mad after Krishna: "My Lord Govinda, because of separation from You, I consider even a moment to be like a great millennium. Tears flow from my eyes like torrents of rain, and I see the entire world as void in Your absence."

The final verse of the *Shikshashtakam* elucidates the highest end in chanting the holy name—losing selfish interest and becoming absorbed in a state of Divine Rapture. This is the result of true

spiritual love. In such an intensely emotional state, the devotee experiences transcendental intimacy, which allows him to address Krishna with loving familiarity: "Let Krishna tightly embrace me, His maidservant, who has fallen at His lotus feet. Let Him trample me or break my heart by not being present before me. He is a debauchee, after all, and can do whatever He likes. But He is still, no matter what, the worshipable Lord of my life."

All these teachings are elaborated upon in the *Shri Chaitanya-charitamrita*, which has been translated and commented on by His Divine Grace A. C. Bhaktivedanta Swami Prabhupada.

Shri Chaitanya-charitamrita *in English, translated and commentated on by His Divine Grace A. C. Bhaktivedanta Swami Prabhupada.*

THE 6 GOSWAMIS

Chaitanya Mahaprabhu experienced divine love, a mysticism of the highest order, and He communicated the confidential essence of this love to His **most intimate followers.** While He meticulously instructed them how to convey His teachings for the word, it was their responsibility to systematize this knowledge and to formulate a method for its wide distribution. After all, how would future generations understand what Mahaprabhu felt? And how would they attempt to recapture the experience? It was the Six Goswamis of Vrindavan who took the challenge to heart, making Mahaprabhu's inner experience accessible.

Raghunath Das Goswami (1495–1571) was the first to meet the Master. He was born in a non-*brahmana* family (which made him distinct among the Six Goswamis) in the town of Chandpur (now Shri Krishnapur), West Bengal. He was extremely wealthy, yet he had a distaste for material riches.

By association with the great saint Haridas Thakur, Raghunath Das anxiously anticipated the day he could see Shri Chaitanya. This occurred shortly after Mahaprabhu took *sannyas*, in 1510, when the young Raghunath Das ran away from home to meet Mahaprabhu in Shantipur. Das Goswami, as Raghunath Das came to be called, became the

preeminent mystic in the Vaishnava tradition and composed beautiful poetry based on his meditations.

In South India, shortly after meeting Raghunath Das Goswami for the first time, Mahaprabhu stayed at the house of Vyenkata Bhatta. At the time Vyenkata had a seven-year-old son named Gopal Bhatta. He would be trained by Mahaprabhu Himself and eventually grow up to be one of the major theologians of Gaudiya Vaishnavism, Gopal Bhatta Goswami (1503–1578). As a South Indian *brahmana*, Gopal Bhatta was keenly aware of the minutiae of day-to-day Vaishnava practice; thus, he would be an invaluable asset to the mission of the Goswamis. Along with Sanatan Goswami, he compiled the "lawbook" for Gaudiya Vaishnavas, called the *Hari-bhakti-vilas*. The book details minute aspects of the tradition, including Deity worship, temple rituals, and Vaishnava etiquette.

Rupa (1489–1564) and Sanatan (1488–1558) Goswamis, also of South Indian roots, were prominent administrators in the Islamic government in Bengal. Both were great scholars and leaders. Shri Chaitanya's wave of devotion swept them up too, and they were introduced to Mahaprabhu when He was on His way to Vrindavan. Later, Rupa met the Master in Prayag (now Allahabad) and received

instruction in *rasa* theology from Him. Sanatan met Mahaprabhu in Benares and there learned from Him the science of *avatars* and the complex philosophy of how God manifests in this world. Rupa and Sanatan were prolific writers. Their contributions included literally dozens of books of drama, poetry, and philosophy.

The work of Rupa and Sanatan was expanded by their young nephew, Jiva Goswami (1513–1598), who is to this day considered one of India's greatest philosophers. He developed themes begun by his renowned uncles and highlighted the nuances of their theological ideals. Some say that Jiva, the youngest of the Six Goswamis, met Shri Chaitanya on only one occasion, as a child. Still, this one meeting, along with the inspiration derived from Rupa and Sanatan, was enough to sustain Jiva throughout his productive career.

Raghunath Bhatta Goswami (1505–1579) offered no literary contribution, but was known for his beautiful singing and for his elaborate recitation of the *Bhagavatam*. Indeed, the essence of Vaishnava theology centers on *kirtan*, the ecstatic singing of the holy name. Raghunath Bhatta Goswami set the highest example by singing the glories of the Lord like no other.

Rupa Goswami and Sanatana Goswami.

BHAKTI
DEVOTIONAL LOVE

The essence of Shri Chaitanya's teaching is *bhakti,* or "devotional love for Krishna." The word itself is derived from either of two Sanskrit roots. The first is *bhanj,* which refers to "separation." This derivation indicates the importance of Vaishnava dualism: one can serve only a God who is "separate" from the self. If the living being is fundamentally one with God, as Advaita Vedantists propose, there is no opportunity for *bhakti,* because *bhakti* implies two entities: the devotee and the one to whom he or she is devoted.

more commonly, *bhakti* is traced to the verbal root *bhaj,* which means "to worship," "to be devoted to" or "to participate in." In the second verse of his famed *sutras* on *bhakti,* Shandilya defines *bhakti* as "exclusive and intense loving attachment to the Lord." The Vaishnava sage Narada elaborates upon this definition in his *Narada-bhakti-sutra,* where he says, "*Bhakti* consists of offering one's every action to the Supreme Lord and feeling extreme distress in forgetting Him." (*Sutra* 19). The very first book of the *Bhagavatam* defines *bhakti* as *parama-dharma,* or "the highest and most satisfying function of the soul." *Bhakti* is thus paramount in Vaishnava thought.

The concept of *bhakti* is found in the writings of the South Indian Alvars, who belonged to India's earliest organized Vaishnava tradition, Shrivaishnavism. And

it is also found in the North, as is amply represented by the works of Rupa Goswami, whose *bhakti-rasa* theology is at the very core of Gaudiya Vaishnavism. *Bhakti* became prominent in 15th- and 16th-century India, which witnessed a "*bhakti* renaissance."

Coincidentally, during this same period the Western world experienced its own renaissance—one that moved in the opposite direction. If the Indian renaissance emphasized devotion to God, the Western one focused on empirical learning and material progress, on science and technology. In essence, Western materialism came to the fore, and spirituality receded to the background.

The European Renaissance is often remembered as a period of growth, a journey toward self-sufficiency and self-discovery. To characterize these times, historian Jules Michelet coined the term "rebirth." Those were times of a newfound awakening, when man was able to escape his preoccupation with religion and superstition and to become truly progressive by focusing on material nature, on the body, and on the world around him. Man moved toward materialistic complexity, leaving spirituality and simple living as a thing of the past.

The *bhakti* renaissance, unlike its Western counterpart, was a move toward minimalism, if also towards essential spiritual truths. Rather than reach for new levels of complexity, this renaissance was concerned with the essential dynamics of the religious impulse; it responded to man's inner need for devotional exchange with his Creator, to man's longing for love.

There were those, however, who held on to ritualistic tradition and resisted the "new ideas" of the *bhakti* reformers, even though the *bhakti* movement drew its premises from the very same texts the traditionalists used.

Nonetheless, most of India has been greatly influenced by *bhakti* and *bhakti*'s practitioners. This may be because *bhakti* speaks to something fundamental in man, and because the opposite—a renaissance moving toward material progress—while advantageous in some ways, ultimately leaves one spiritually barren, without a soul.

"Holy places baffle sensible people... In important aspects their existence is on the level of the mind, or of emotion, or of the utterly transcendent."
—Norvin Hein
Professor Emeritus of Religion,
Yale University

SACRED PLACES

7

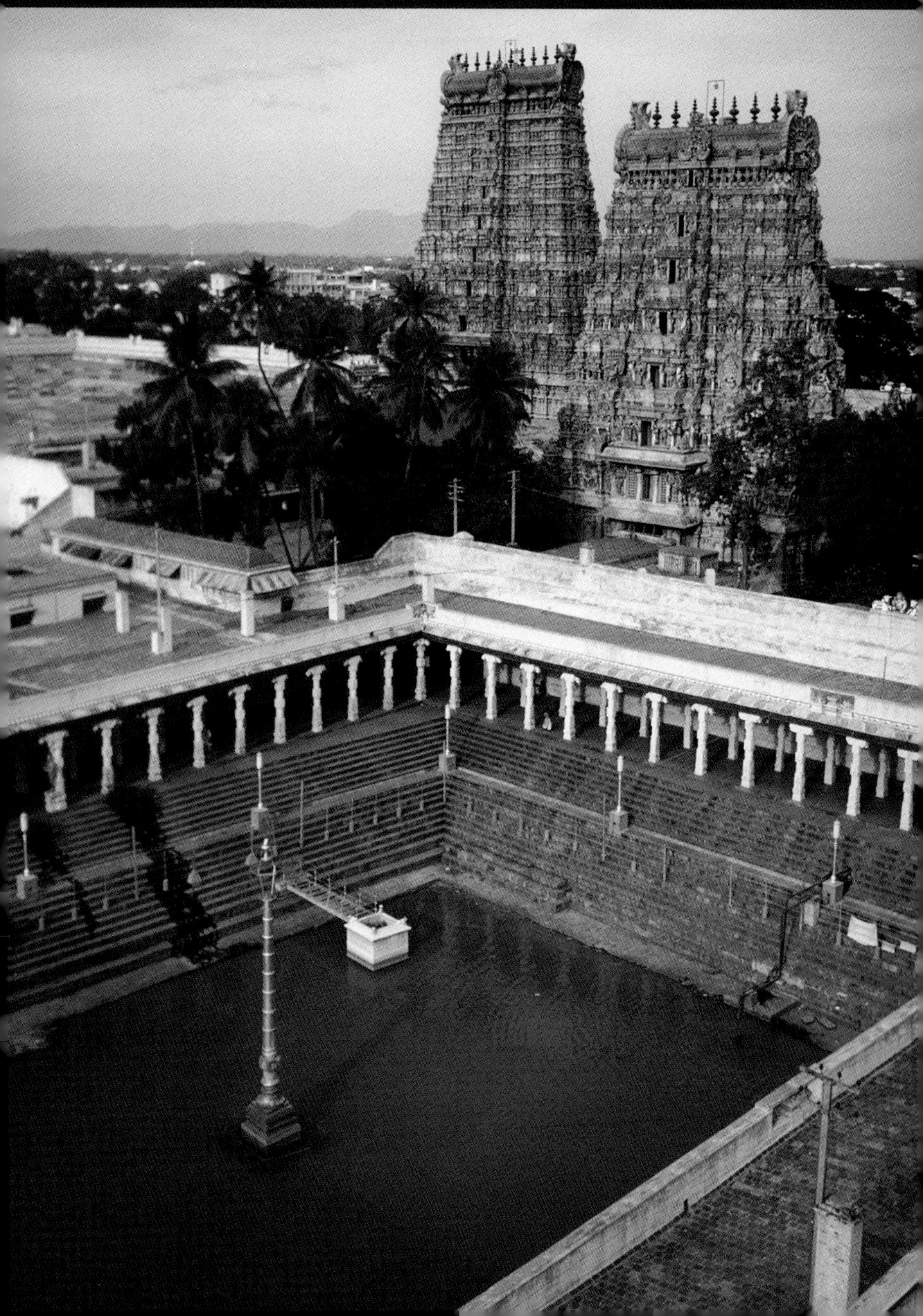

Temples

Reclining image of Vishnu outside a Vaishnava temple.

Like the cathedrals of France or the Vatican in Rome, Vaishnava temples evoke a sense of awe. At the same time, they also evoke a sense of intimate association with the Divine.

The late scholar Mircea Eliade has analyzed the structural significance of Indian temples:

"[Such] temples… are explicitly recapitulations of the body. The symbolic blueprint of a temple is the Vastu-purusha Mandala, a diagram drawn on its future site. This diagram incorporates the directions, the lunar mansions, the planets, the [demi]gods, and the human body and symbolically transmits their forms to the temple rising above it. Indian architectural manuals explicitly liken the temple to the body: the door is the mouth; the dome above the spire is the head. Just as the human skull has a suture, from which the soul at death departs to heaven, so also the dome is pierced with a finial; and the inner sanctum of the temple is the place of the soul within the human body…. Because the…temple represents a human body, the journey into the temple is also a journey within oneself. Contact with the image of divinity in the heart of the temple is the symbolic replication of the meeting of divinity within the center of one's being."[1]

The "divinity in the heart of the temple" refers to the special feature of Vaishnava worship: the Lord's personal presence on the altar in a form of a Deity (archa-vigraha). The Deity is considered God Himself, a type of avatar, known as archa-avatar. According to the Shrimad Bhagavatam (11.27.12), God in the form of the archa-avatar can incarnate in any of eight material elements: stone, wood, metal, earth, paint, sand, jewels, or the mind. The tradition is clear: in order to be recognized as worshipable forms of the Deity, these elements must be "infused with divine presence" by a specially trained priest, and the sacred images must be fashioned according to precise dimensions outlined in scripture.

Once the Deity is established in the temple, the daily activities of the Lord are reenacted on the altar: in the early morning the priests awaken the Deity and offer Him breakfast, while chanting special

mantras. At midday the priests serve an elaborate lunch, after which the Deity takes a short nap. Then they place on the altar various kinds of paraphernalia for the Deity's pleasure. In the evening, they offer Him a large feast, on a par with His midday meal, and chant mantras for His evening rest.

The altar activities are performed by trained priests while worshipers come to see ("to take *darshan* of") the beautiful form of the Lord on the altar. Devotees chant mantras, sing the glories of the Deity, admire His beautifully decorated form, and offer prayers.

Vaishnava temples take adherents beyond the impersonal concepts of divinity and enable entrance into God's personhood. God in His many manifestations—Rama, Vishnu, Nrisimha, Jagannath, Krishna—offers *darshan* to all, in thousands of temples worldwide.

Notes

1. 'Sacred space,' in "The Encyclopedia of Religion," ed., Mircea Eliade. 1987. New York: Macmillan Publishing Company. Vol. 12, p. 532.

SACRED ARCHITECTURE

India has an ancient architectural tradition. The principles of this tradition are delineated throughout the Puranas and other scriptures, most notably the Shilpa-shastra (compiled by Vishvakarma, architect of the gods) and the *Vastu-shastra*. In addition, the *Shulba-sutras* contain geometrical details for setting up places for sacrifices (*yagyas*). Basically, three styles of temple architecture have emerged.

In northern and western districts, most favored is the *nagara* style: tall buildings with large pointed steeples over the *garbha-griha*, or that portion of the temple where the Deity is housed. Such temples usually include a veranda-type area, used as an audience hall, where worshipers can circumambulate the Deity.

The eastern style favors a more rounded tower along with a complex of buildings, usually with separate areas for singers and dancers, for dramatic performers, and for worshipers of various deities.

The southern style is known for its distinct *gopuras*—elegant, elaborately carved structures that tower over the entrance gates of the temple complex.

Vaishnava temples are constructed according to elaborate mathematical calculations, incorporating a geometric yogic form (the Vastu Purusha Mandala, as seen above) that serves to sanctify the structure.

VRINDAVAN
THE HOLY LAND of BRAJ

In the North Indian state of Uttar Pradesh, 85 miles south of New Delhi, lies a bucolic area of land known as Braj, or Vraja (literally "pasture"). Its pastoral atmosphere is inviting to all who journey to this holiest of Vaishnava pilgrimage sites.

The villages of Braj spread over an area about 40 miles in diameter. This area includes the city of Mathura and twelve main forests (one of which is Vrindavan, often known as the spiritual center of Braj), along with 125 secondary forests.

It is misleading, however, to think of Braj merely in terms of its geographical location; this would undermine its spiritual significance.

To Vaishnavas, Braj is sacred space. It has a polydimensional nature that places it within time and space and beyond it as well. Lord Krishna's eternal play (lila) in the spiritual realm is from time to time revealed in the world of three dimensions. When it is so revealed, as it was 5,000 years ago, it manifests itself in Braj. For this reason Vaishnavas refer to the spiritual realm also as Braj.

Thus, we have the celestial Braj (the one in heaven) and the terrestrial Braj (the one on earth): Vaishnavas see both manifestations as equal.

Vaishnava scriptures contend that the celestial Braj (and the other spiritual domains that extend from it) is the original home of all living beings, from which they were separated at creation's dawn. Thus from the beginning of time man has yearned for a perfect home—a paradise, a Shangri-La, a Walden—where he could return to his original idyllic state of peace and happiness. The terrestrial Braj, with its small village conclave of holy men and temples, fulfills this aspiration for all who embrace its shelter.

One best experiences Braj directly, by going on *parikrama* (tour, pilgrimage) with one who is familiar

with the terrain, both its geography and its inner meaning. The sand of Braj, once walked upon by Radha and Krishna, is thought to be imbued with love of the divine. Thus, it is not uncommon to see pilgrims reverentially take sand and put it to their heads.

The multiplicity of holy lands on earth and the world's many religions accommodate seekers who might have diverse mentalities and inclinations. Pilgrims go to holy places for a host of reasons: to cure physical or emotional ills, to pray for wealth or material prosperity. Some are inexplicably drawn for reasons unknown even to themselves. A good number make the

journey to enhance and provoke the internal progress of the spirit. Braj inspires the highest of these motivations. Indeed, of the seven traditional pilgrimage sites in India that are said to award everything from *bhukti* ("material benefit") to *mukti* ("liberation"), only Braj offers *bhakti* and *prema*, or devotion and love for the Supreme Being.

I NEVER FORGET BRAJ

Uddhava, I never forget Braj,
Vrindavan, Gokul, the forests,
bowers, and the shade of dense groves.

Seeing Mother Yashoda and
Nanda at dawn, I feel happy.
Bearing warm bread and butter,
they feed Me with great love.
I play in the company
of the cowherd boys,
and pass every day in laughter.

Uddhava, I never forget Braj,
the beautiful banks of the Yamuna
and the shade of the groves.
Here are the wish-fulfilling cows,
there the calves, there the pots,
and there the milksheds
where they are milked.
Once, when the cowherd
boys got together,
they created an uproar,
dancing and wrestling.

This Mathura here is
a city of gold, jewels and pearls.
But when memories of
Braj come, they bring joy,
and the heart overflows and
cannot be contained by the body.

I engaged in countless types of
pastimes continually,
and Yashoda and
Nanda tolerated it.
After saying this,
Sur's master fell silent
And became remorseful.

— *Surdas, a 15th-century poet and saint*
(in Krishna's voice)

NAVADVIP

Navadvip is situated about 65 miles north of Kolkata (Calcutta), connected to it by road, river, and rail. This unassuming village environment is famous as the birthplace of Shri Chaitanya (1486–1533), who is also known as Gaur (the "golden" incarnation).

Shri Chaitanya is nondifferent from Shri Krishna, hence Navadvip (Mayapur) and Vrindavan, though geographically different, are regarded as identical abodes, and the lila of Gaura (Chaitanya) and that of Krishna are mystically connected. Vaishnavas reverently refer to the thirty-two-mile Navadvip/Mayapur region as Gaura-mandala.

In 1063 C.E., Navadvip became the capital of Bengal under the Hindu rule of Lakshmana Sena, but in 1202 it was conquered and destroyed by Muhammed Bakhtiar Khilji. Bengal then passed under Islamic rule. Despite social friction, Hindus and Muslims lived there together. Navadvip, which was a famous seat of Sanskrit learning, became a stronghold of orthodox brahmanism. It was into this environment that Shri Chaitanya appeared.

Literally hundreds of sites connected to Shri Chaitanya Mahaprabhu's pastimes are found throughout the area. The Yoga-pitha, where Mahaprabhu was born, today houses deities of Him and His associates, and pilgrims daily visit the area. Nearby is Shrivas Angan,

the house of Shrivas Thakur, where Shri Chaitanya inaugurated the Sankirtan movement, or the religious movement based on the singing and dancing in glorification of Krishna's holy names.

Historically, Navadvip is considered to have been an area consisting of nine (nava) islands (dvipa). The "nine islands," many believe, refer to nine spiritual islands to be perceived only by those who have attained the topmost realization, because

these islands, as such, are nowhere to be found. Pilgrims generally tour the area of "nine islands"—which are, to external vision, merely nine towns, located right next to each other—in the following sequence: Antardvip, Simantadvip, Godrumdvip, Madhyadvip, Koladvip, Ritudvip, Jahnudvip, Modadrumdvip, and Rudradvip.

In an esoteric sense, the islands correspond to the nine processes of devotional service: hearing about God, chanting of Him, remembering Him, serving His lotus feet, worshiping Him, praying to Him, assisting Him, befriending Him, and sacrificing everything for Him.

THE REDISCOVERY OF SHRI CHAITANYA'S BIRTHPLACE

By the 19th century, the importance of Lord Chaitanya's life and mission had been largely forgotten; Muslim conquerors and the passage of time had all but obliterated Shri Chaitanya from history. This was soon to be corrected by a single individual named Bhaktivinode Thakur (1838–1914). An avid follower of Chaitanya's teachings, Bhaktivinode set out to rediscover the Lord's birthplace.

To Bhaktivinode's surprise, the village that his contemporaries knew to be Navadvip was only one hundred years old and could not possibly be the same Navadvip in which Shri Chaitanya had appeared. There were diverse opinions, and some said that the Lord's birthplace was now under the Ganges, which since the 15th century had changed its course.

But Bhaktivinode was relentless, and he soon heard of a place northeast of the town then considered Navadvip. Bhaktivinode soon realized that this other place—an old Muslim-governed village—was the actual Navadvip (Mayapur), and he sought to confirm this theory with available evidence. Strong proof came from two maps made by British pilots who had navigated the Ganges.

Bhaktivinode found important leads also in regional scriptures. For example, in Narahari Chakravarti's Bhakti-ratnakara he read that the courtyard of Shrivas Pandit, where Shri Chaitanya inaugurated the congregational chanting of the maha-mantra, was situated one hundred dhanus (200 yards) to the north of the "House of God."

The courtyard of Shrivas still exists, as it did in Shri Chaitanya's time (and in Bhaktivinode's as well); it was thus relatively easy to determine the site of Shri Chaitanya's birth. This information aided Bhaktivinode in his discovery of Shri Chaitanya's birth site. The evidence was tallied, and it was augmented by further geographical and archeological studies made by Bhaktivinode himself.

In an attempt to get spiritual confirmation of the site's authenticity, Bhaktivinode brought to the area his old and ailing teacher, Jagannath das Babaji. Babaji Maharaj, although incapacitated, began to jump in ecstasy and cry profusely in love of God. Such an outpouring of divine love convinced Bhaktivinode, perhaps even more than the hard, external evidence, that this was indeed Shri Chaitanya's birthplace.

Mayapur
A Tradition Continues

The significance of Shri Chaitanya to the Vaishnava tradition is inestimable. After Bhaktivinode Thakur discovered the area of Shri Chaitanya's birth, a prominent successor in the tradition, His Divine Grace A. C. Bhaktivedanta Swami Prabhupada, sought to preserve and enhance the area as a pilgrimage site by constructing a magnificent temple complex. The work began in 1972 and continues to the present day.

The temple complex, now known as the Shri Mayapur Chandrodaya Mandir, includes a grand temple, a beautifully maintained park, a school, a library, a museum, a memorial to Shrila Prabhupada, an auditorium, guesthouses, and more. It is able to accommodate hundreds of guests and is the primary focus for the glorification of Shri Chaitanya in the area. This devotional complex is still being developed, and when completed it will fulfill Bhaktivinode's dream—a vision he had when Mayapur was a simple village.

One evening, Bhaktivinode was sitting in his home at Godrumdvip in Mayapur, looking out over the verdant fields beyond the clear waters of the Jalangi River. In the distance he saw a brilliant effulgence emanating from one particular direction. Focusing on what he saw, Bhaktivinode realized it was a vision of a golden city, a spiritual city that would take shape in the near future. It was a city dedicated to the glorification of Shri Chaitanya, and inhab-

Bhaktivinode Thakur

ited by people of all races and religious affiliations. "After all," Bhaktivinode reasoned, "Lord Chaitanya did not make his advent to liberate a mere few men in India. His objective was to liberate all living entities of all countries and throughout the entire universe, and to preach eternal, nonsectarian religious principles."

Bhaktivinode longingly expressed his desire to see that happen: "Oh, for that day when the fortunate English, French, Russian, German, and American people will take up

Shrila Bhaktisiddhanta Saraswati Thakur with devotees at Mayapur.

banners, *mridangas* [drums], and *kartals* [cymbals] and raise *kirtan* [devotional singing] through their streets and towns."

"The time will come," Bhaktivinode wrote, "when in the land of Navadvip, on the plain of the Ganges, a magnificent temple will arise, proclaiming to the world the glories of Lord Chaitanya." He also wrote of a great personality, who would soon take birth to fulfill these dreams.

Some sixty years later, in 1971, Shrila Prabhupada, while living in Mayapur in a thatched hut with several disciples, spoke of Bhaktivinode's dream of a holy city and of a marble palace yet to come. He described comfortable accommodation for guests and devotees, parks with elephants, deer, and peacocks, food distribution for the poor, schools, and a magnificent temple, and much more. This was his vision, and today his followers are working to see it develop to its full potential. In fact, Prabhupada himself was obviously the great personality predicted by Bhaktivinode, as mentioned above. He inspired his disciples, personally oversaw the development of the project—down to its most minute details—and in his lifetime turned

some vacant fields into a large and vibrant spiritual center that put Mayapur back on the map. He brought thousands of English, French, German, and American people to raise *kirtan* together with *mridangas*, banners, and *kartals*. And he directed his disciples to continue to fulfill Bhaktivinode's vision.

Bhaktivinode Thakur (opposite page) rediscovered Mayapur, as described on the previous pages. Shrila Prabhupada (above) built upon his work by constructing the international complex known as Shri Mayapur Chandrodaya Mandir (below).

The Ganges

Hindus everywhere hold **sacred** the Ganges, perhaps the best known river on earth. Practitioners of the Vaishnava tradition regard it second in terms of holiness only to the Yamuna, which is directly associated with Lord Krishna.

Beginning high in the snowy Himalayas, the sacred waters of the Ganges flow eastward through the Vindhya range. The river joins with the Yamuna at Allahabad and continues eastward until it reaches the Bay of Bengal.

of it, swim in it, and are apparently not affected....Perhaps bacteriophage [a bacteria-destroying virus normally present in sewage] renders the river sterile." Whatever the reason, the Ganges remains pure—and purifying—for all who bathe in its waters.

Saints and sages have for millennia bathed in the Ganges, renowned for its purity. This is so despite the fact that people wash, litter, and defecate directly in the river. Although presently the Ganges is exposed to chemical waste and a variety of pollutants, experts insist that its waters are pure.

For example, Dr. John Howard Northrup, a co-winner of the Nobel Prize for Chemistry in 1946, has said, "We know the Ganges is highly contaminated. Yet Indians drink out

Even as recently as 1999, Professor Charles Wilcott, a marine biologist and Indologist, looked at Ganges water and concluded, "There is something mystical about Ganges water, something that separates it from ordinary liquid with the same or similar chemical composition....My findings point to an extraordinary phenomenon when it comes to the Ganges."

THE GANGES COMES TO EARTH

According to the ancient Vedic cosmological scheme, there are three planetary systems in this universe: the upper, or heavenly planets (not to be confused with the kingdom of God); the middle planets, including earth; and the lower, or hellish planets. The entire universe is enclosed in an immense shell, millions of miles thick, beyond which lies the spiritual world. Early traditions assert that the Ganges originates from beyond the shell of the material world.

The *Shrimad Bhagavatam* relates that once, long ago, a king named Bali conquered all three planetary systems. He ousted the demigods from their heavenly domains and installed himself as the king of heaven. Aditi, the mother of the demigods, aggrieved at her sons' defeat, fasted and prayed to Lord Krishna for twelve consecutive days. The Lord became pleased with her and agreed to reinstate the demigods by incarnating as Vamanadeva, a dwarf *brahmana* mendicant.

Lord Vamanadeva approached Bali Maharaj and begged him for a mere three paces of land. When Bali agreed, with two steps Vamanadeva covered the entire universe, thus reclaiming the demigods' lost property. While taking His second step, Vamanadeva kicked a hole in the universal shell with His toe, and a few drops of water from the Karana Ocean leaked into the universe. This water became the Ganges River. The Ganges is considered sacred and purifying, both because it comes from the spiritual world and because it touched the toe of Lord Vamanadeva.

At first, the Ganges flowed only in the heavenly planets. Then a great earthly king named Bhagiratha, a devotee of Lord Vishnu, desired to have the Ganges purify the earth and prayed for the river to descend. The Ganges personified appeared before King Bhagirath and agreed to fulfill his desire. But she had a reservation.

"When I fall from the sky to the surface of the planet earth," she explained, "the water will certainly be very forceful. Who will sustain that force? If I am not sustained, I shall pierce the surface of the earth, and then I shall glide down to the hellish planets."

The Ganges asked King Bhagirath to find someone willing and able to break her fall. To satisfy the Ganges, King Bhagirath prayed to the powerful Lord Shiva, asking him to catch the falling Ganges water on his head. Lord Shiva agreed.

Since that time, Lord Shiva has been sustaining the Ganges on his head, and its sacred waters have been flowing on the earth. The Himalayan mountain and glacier from which the Ganges flows are still named after King Bhagirath.

According to the Vedic literature, anyone who bathes in the Ganges is cleansed of all material contamination and becomes eligible to be liberated in this lifetime. He may then return to the eternal spiritual world, where the Ganges originates.

JAGANNATH
PURI

On the east coast of India, in the province of Orissa, amid palm trees and pristine beaches, lies the city of Puri. It is shaped like the silhouette of a conchshell and is renowned as the **home of Lord Jagannath**, a manifestation of Krishna in the form of holy wood. Pilgrims from all over India come to pay homage to this manifestation of the Lord, housed in one of India's most famous temples.

The temple, sometimes referred to as "Shri Mandir," is situated on what was once elevated ground known as Nilgiri, "the blue hill." The present temple was constructed under the patronage of King Chadoganga Deva in the 12th century. Refurbished more than a dozen times, the temple still stands where the original temple stood.

The central shrine of the temple is typical of Oriyan architecture. It consists of a miniature kingdom of four buildings, known as (1) the Bhoga Mandap, where fifty-four food offerings are prepared daily for the deities; (2) the Nata Mandap, a large dancing hall for the Lord's pleasure; (3) the Mukhasala, where the Lord gives His darshan, or "audience," for all of His devotees; and (4) the Bada-deula, or the area of the main temple.

The temple is 65 meters (215 feet) in height—the tallest in all of Puri, and, in fact, all of Orissa.

The ornate, magnificently carved gates that surround the temple are unique. The eastern gate is called "The Lion Gate," and the gates on the southern, northern, and western sides are called the gates of the Horse, Elephant, and Tiger. Through these gates throng the multitudes for a glimpse of Lord Jagannath.

Lord Jagannath, a form of Krishna, stands about five feet tall. On His right side is Subhadra, His sister (a manifestation of His mystic potency Yogamaya), and on her right stands their elder brother Baladeva (Jagannath's immediate expansion).

The deities appear immense, inspiring awe and devotion. Many residents of Puri come every day to see them and get the *mahaprasad*—food offered to the deities that feeds thousands every day. But the real nourishment in Puri is spiritual, for everyone there feeds on the energy of Lord Jagannath.

Baladeva, Subhadra, and Jagannath.

The ancient Jagannath temple, a major pilgrimage site in Eastern India.

THE FESTIVAL OF THE CHARIOTS

With the exception of the Kumbha Mela, the annual Ratha-yatra festival ("The Festival of the Chariots") attracts the largest gathering of pilgrims in India. At this festival, the deities of **Jagannath, Baladeva,** and Subhadra (described on the previous page) are taken out of the Jagannath temple and placed on three giant carts constructed specifically for the festival parade.

Jagannath's own cart projects fifty feet into the sky, and is about thirty-six feet wide, which makes it a formidable "juggernaut" ("Jagannath", in fact, is the origin of the word. Sixteen large wheels help glide the cart down the road. Jagannath's cart is followed by two slightly smaller carts—one for Baladeva and one for Subhadra.

Several hundred priests attend to the deities and the three carts as the carts are pulled through thronging crowds. Each cart has four ropes, and during the festival the ropes are pulled by nearly 5,000 people. Millions follow along in the summer heat, and praises of Jagannath permeate the sky: "Jaya Jagannath! All glories to the Lord of the universe!" The procession continues for two miles until the parade arrives at the Lord's pavilion, the Gundicha Temple. Seven days later, enacted with all the pomp and vigor of the initial first festival, a second festival ensues, signifying the return of the Lord to the Jagannath temple. Poets and artists alike have sought to depict the majesty of the parade and the beauty of Jagannath. Below are several popular verses describing the sweetness of Lord Jagannath and emphasizing His identity as Shri Krishna.

1. Sometimes in great happiness Lord Jagannath, with His flute, makes a loud concert in the groves on the banks of the Yamuna. He is like a bumblebee who tastes the beautiful lotuslike faces of the cowherd girls of Braj. May that Jagannath Swami be the object of my vision.

2. In His left hand Jagannath holds a flute. On His head He wears the feathers of peacocks, and on His hips He wears fine yellow silken cloth. Out of the corners of His eyes He bestows sidelong glances upon His loving devotees. May that Jagannath Swami be the object of my vision.

3. When Lord Jagannath is on His Ratha-yatra cart and is moving along the road, at every step there is a loud presentation of prayers and songs chanted by large assemblies of *brahmanas*. Hearing their hymns, Lord Jagannath is favorably disposed toward them. He is the ocean of mercy and the true friend of all the worlds. May that Jagannath Swami be the object of my vision.

The Inner Meaning of Ratha-yatra

Although Lord Krishna became a great king in His time, His childhood He spent in the village of Vrindavan. There He sported with the cowherd boys and girls, and of all of them, Radharani was His most beloved.

But when Krishna left Vrindavan to become king of Dvaraka, Shrimati Radharani's lamentation was unequaled in the universe. She never gave up hope that He would someday return to Her. In this way She enjoys a special transcendental longing known as *vipralambha-bhava*, or "the mood of love-in-separation."

Once, while Krishna was king, He met Radharani and Her friends in a secluded place at Kurukshetra, a place of pilgrimage in north central India. But when Radharani saw Krishna in His princely garb, with full opulence and regalia, She longed to see Him as the simple cowherd boy She once knew. She longed to bring Him back to Vrindavan.

This mood of wanting to bring Krishna back to the intimacy of Vrindavan is the confidential theme of the Ratha-yatra festival. When devotees pull the long, sturdy ropes of the Ratha-yatra cart, they are pulling Krishna back into their hearts—back to the land of Vrindavan.

Radha and Krishna incarnated as Chaitanya Mahaprabhu, and in this way, They

were reunited—in His body. Yet during His last years, which He spent in Jagannath Puri, Lord Chaitanya fully manifested the mood of Radharani and relentlessly lamented the divine tragedy of Radha and Krishna's separation.

Every year in Jagannath Puri, Lord Chaitanya celebrated the Ratha-yatra festival in Radharani's mood of pulling Krishna back to the simple, villagelike atmosphere of Vrindavan. Mahaprabhu taught that this feeling of separation actually evokes the presence of Krishna and, ultimately, gives way to the highest happiness. This is the internal meaning of Ratha-yatra.

TRAVEL Information

In the preceding section, we have highlighted a small sampling of the sacred places one finds throughout the subcontinent of India. For most Indians, important sites are the Saptapuris, "the Seven Cities," also known as Mokshapuris ("the cities that award liberation"). These are Ayodhya, Mathura, Haridwar, Benares, Kanchi, Ujjain, and Dwarka. Indian texts also focus on seven sacred rivers: the Ganges, Yamuna, Godavari, Sarasvati, Narmada, Sindhu, and Kaveri.

The most important pilgrimage sites for Gaudiya Vaishnavas, however, are Braj (Vrindavan), Mayapur, and Jagannath Puri. Although holy places can ultimately be reached only by internal meditation and intense devotion, one may begin one's journey by exploring these external manifestations of the spiritual realm. So here we offer basic travel data: maps, and information about trains, major places to stay, and sacred temples.

Braj (Vrindavan)

Braj has more than five thousand temples, the most important of which are the temples of Madan-mohan, Govindadev, Radha-Raman, Radha-Gokulananda, Radha-Damodar, Banki-behari, Radhavallabha, Jugal Kishor, Radha-Gopinath, Radha Shyamasundar, and Krishna-Balaram. Other major pilgrimage sites include Radha-kunda, Govardhan Hill, and Lord Krishna's birthplace at Mathura.

New Delhi to Mathura: Mathura, the small city closely associated with Braj, is 140 kilometers (85 miles) south of Delhi, and getting there by taxi takes about three hours. Travel by train (such as the Taj Express, which leaves regularly from Delhi's Nizamuddin Station and goes directly to Mathura Junction) will shorten the trip by about one hour. Mathura is just ten kilometers (six miles) south of Vrindavan region, and getting there by autorikshaw usually takes just over half an hour (a little less by taxi).

Places to Stay: The ISKCON guesthouse in Vrindavan has many Western amenities and is a convenient place to stay. Maheshwari Ashram is inexpensive and comfortable, as is Jai Singh Gera at Radha-Raman. In Mathura, there are accommodations at the Agra Hotel and at Radha Ashok.

ISKCON: The Chakra building is economical, while the Lotus building is more costly but offers nicer accommodation. ISKCON Mayapur has several more guest buildings—the Gada building, the Shankh building, the Vamsi building—with literally hundreds of rooms, affording excellent accommodation. For further information, please visit www.mayapur.info.

Mayapur

In Mayapur one can find sacred places connected to the pastimes of Shri Chaitanya and His associates, particularly Shri Chaitanya's birthplace. Several ruins from Shri Chaitanya's time are prominent tourist attractions as well, and some have been refurbished by the Archeological Survey of India. Most important: On any given day you'll find ten or twenty luxury buses from Calcutta and elsewhere parked in the ISKCON Mayapur parking lot. The main attraction in Mayapur is the ISKCON temple complex.

Kolkata to Navadvip/Mayapur:

Mayapur is 120 kilometers (75 miles) north of Kolkata. Although a taxi is probably the best way to get there, many pilgrims take trains from Sheáldah and Howrah stations to Krishnagar or Navadvip. From Navadvip one takes a short rickshaw ride to the Mayapur boat crossing. A low boat awaits pilgrims on the shore. After crossing the Ganges, one arrives on the outskirts of Mayapur. Another short rickshaw ride leaves one in Mayapur proper. An alternate route is the Kamrup Express, which involves a similar journey. There is also an early-morning bus that leaves for Mayapur from the Esplanade bus stand in downtown Kolkata, but this is a somewhat longer ride, because the bus makes many local stops. One can also take "The Mayapur Bus," run by ISKCON; it goes to and from Kolkata daily.

Places to Stay: The Janbhi-

tirtha Hotel is located in the center of Mayapur. The best accommodations in Mayapur, however, are those offered by

Jagannath Puri

Puri is the home of Lord Jagannath and the place where Shri Chaitanya spent the final eighteen years of His life. A tropical seaside area of great beauty, Puri is also a haven for spiritual seekers.

Bhubaneshwar to Puri: The nearest

airport to Puri is Bhubaneshwar, 60 kilometers (37 miles) away. Indian Airlines flies to Bhubaneshwar from Delhi, Kolkata, Hyderabad, Chennai (Madras), and Mumbai (Bombay).

To go to Puri from Delhi, one can take the Neelachal Express, a train that makes the trip in less than 32 hours. The Howrah–Puri Express, which leaves from Kolkata, takes about 11 hours. Buses from both Delhi and Kolkata to Bhubaneshwar are generally faster than the trains. The journey from Bhubaneshwar to Puri takes about two hours by train or bus.

Places to Stay: Puri receives a good deal

of tourist attention throughout the year and has many hotels, youth hostels, and ashrams. The northeast section, just off Chakra Tirtha Road, is home to a number of budget hotels. The most popular is the Puri Hotel, situated in the main Indian tourist area, near Beach Sea Road. The Nilachal Ashok and the Mayfair Beach Resort offer the highest quality accommodation.

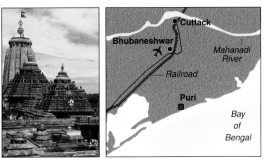

"Among the traditions of Krishna worship ... the relation of the aesthetic and the religious has been most explicitly elaborated. Nowhere else... has the aesthetic been so prominent as in Krishna devotion, for Krishna has been represented as supremely alluring, and each of the arts has been employed to make his beauty manifest."

—Donna M. Wulff

Associate Professor of Religious Studies,
Brown University

Fɪne ARTS

For Vaishnavas, art and yoga coalesce. In general, yoga advocates subjugation of the senses, a withdrawal from sensual experience. However, Vaishnavas employ the process of bhakti-yoga, in which the senses are engaged in the pursuit of the divine. Along these lines, author Ananda Coomaraswamy (1877–1947), long the curator of Indian art at the Boston Museum of Fine Arts, states that artistic inspiration in India is generally derived "from the spirit of adoration—the loving and passionate devotion to a personal divinity." He points out that in India the very purpose of "the lover" (i.e., the artist) is to "establish a personal relationship with the Beloved" (i.e., God), and that the "plastic symbol" (i.e., the artwork) is created for this end.

It is no wonder, then, that artistic expression, such as painting and sculpture, would find a prominent place in the Vaishnava world. In fact, Vaishnavas have been referred to as "aesthetic ascetics"—yogis who appreciate the place of beauty in nurturing a relationship to divinity. The vivid and detailed pastimes of Krishna recounted in the *Bhagavata Purana* and the *Gita-govinda* of Jayadeva have provided the inspiration for countless Krishnaite sculptures and paintings over the course of Indian history.

The earliest extant sculptures depicting the Krishna theme are simple, elementary forms composed mainly of stone, and dating back to the Kushana period in Mathura (2nd–3rd centuries C.E.). In later centuries, sculptors in South India expanded their source of materials to include metal, terra-cotta, and wood. Perhaps the greatest period of Indian sculpture, and art in general, was the classical, or Gupta, period (4th–6th centuries C.E.). The late eminent Indologist A. L. Basham writes, "Guptan sculpture

of enraptured expression, depicting Krishna as the divine lover. Their sources of inspiration were, again, the *Shrimad Bhagavatam* and the *Gita-govinda* of Jayadeva.

Twentieth-century artists Jamini Roy and George Keyt are forerunners in the development of modern Krishnaite painting. Roy has produced hundreds of paintings of Krishna as flute-player and dancer, and Keyt has rendered paintings and line drawings of themes from the *Gita-govinda*. Among the foremost modern Krishnaite artists are B. G. Sharma, whose depictions of Krishna are perhaps the most popular of the genre, and the artists of ISKCON's "neo-Vedic" art academy, which has blended traditional themes with the styles of the European masters.

suggests serenity, security, and certainty. It was at this time that India produced some of her most truly religious art."

India enjoyed a rich renaissance of painting during the reign of the Moghul dynasty. At this time, even some of the Muslim rulers were great supporters of Vaishnava art. In particular, Emperor Akbar (1556–1605) commissioned artists to illustrate the celebrated *Ramayana* and *Mahabharata*, among other classics. During this period, Indian miniatures rose to new heights of sophistication.

In the 1680s, Raj Kirpal Pal, the king of Basohli state, sponsored Vaishnava artists. Thus a new school developed. Depictions of Krishna as the butter thief, Krishna sporting with the *gopis*, Krishna on the lap of Mother Yashoda, Krishna the lover of Radha, exhibited great emotional intensity.

In the 18th century, the painters of the Kangra state produced works

POETRY

"Sweet, sweet is my dear Lord's form,
Sweeter still His face, so fair,
But His honey-scented gentle smile
Is sweet beyond compare." — Bilvamangala

One of Krishna's many names is Uttamashloka—"the one who is to be praised with the most choice, poetic words." The scriptures therefore compare Krishna's hue to that of a dark raincloud, His eyes to lotuses, and His effulgent toenails to soothing autumn moons. Without poetic language and spiritual realization, said Shri Chaitanya, it is impossible to describe spiritual subjects.

One example of spiritual poetic insight is found in the verses of Jayadeva, a 12th-century poet-saint. Jayadeva's *Gita-govinda* consists of intimate revelations, or vibrant outpourings of love for Radha and Krishna. Mirabai, a 16th-century *bhakti* poetess, praises Krishna with an intense love and spiritual fervor. Other important Vaishnava poets include Andal and Nammalvar (9th and 10th century, respectively), Bilvamangala (11th century), Chandidas (14th century), Surdas, Rupa Goswami, and Kavi Karnapura (16th century), and Narottam das Thakur (17th century).

Though most of the poets listed

above wrote in regional languages, such as Braj-bhasha or Bengali, they all drew upon Kavya, classical Sanskrit poetics. This supplied them with a rich array of literary devices, such as alliteration (*anupras*) and rhyme (*antanupras*), as well as metaphor, simile, and double-entendre—all centered on Krishna.

The earliest Vaishnava poetry, such as that found in the *Shrimad Bhagavatam*, is written in Sanskrit. Later Sanskrit literature gave birth to a specific poetic style known as the *stotra* (a word derived from the verbal root *stu-*, meaning "to praise, laud, eulogize, extol, celebrate in song or hymn"). The *stotra*, along with several other literary genres, such as the *champu* (a blend of verse and prose), is now a well-established means of conveying devotional love-poetry in India. Whatever the language or style of presentation, Vaishnava poetry points to a conclusion that was best articulated ages ago by an unknown Krishnaite poet: "O Krishna, without You, everything is dark!"

RASA THEOLOGY:
The Poetics of Sacred Relationship

A key component in Vaishnava poetry is the concept of *rasa*. Although there are subtle nuances of difference in the way the word is defined in the natural sciences (e.g., *Ayurveda*), in poetics and in theology it is generally understood to mean "taste" or "savor." Its meaning can also be extended to "dramatic sentiment" or "aesthetic enjoyment."

One of the earliest references to the word *rasa* is in the *Taittiriya Upanishad*, which states, *raso vai sah:* "Ultimate reality is embodied in spiritual aesthetic experience." To explore what this means in relation to the dramatic or poetic arts, we would need to look at an early form of *rasa* theory found in Bharata's *Natya-shastra*. Here, the theory was based on a simple premise: if an emotion arises in a particular environment, producing certain responses and gestures, then a re-creation of that environment and an imitation of those responses and gestures would reproduce a similar emotion in the sensitive and cultured viewer (and no less in the actor). Such a cultured viewer was known as a *rasika*, or one who could relish the true flavor or emotion of a given dramatic performance.

In the 9th century, Anandavardhana took Bharata's idea further, applying it to poetry and all aesthetic experience. In the 11th century, Abhinavagupta expanded the concepts of predecessor aestheticians and made the important connection between aesthetic experience and religious transformation. In the same century, this was brought even further by Bhoja, who emphasized the pre-eminence of *madhurya-rasa*, or the sentiment of conjugal love. By the 12th century compositions like Jayadeva's *Gita-govinda* began to appear, using the methodology and terminology of aesthetic theory and poetics.

The Six Goswamis of Vrindavan (16th century) recognized the terminology and categories of *rasa* theory as ideal for expressing realizations and understandings of divine reality that would otherwise be difficult to convey. Rupa Goswami, especially, brought the *rasa* theory to new heights. In Rupa's perspective, the cultured *rasika* viewer is replaced by the *rasika bhakta*, the seasoned devotee of Krishna, and the play into which he enters is the eternal play of *krishna-lila*, not a fictitious drama conceived by men. The love for Krishna (*krishna-rati*) is understood as the dominant feeling (*sthayi-bhava*) of devotion, a feeling that constitutes a permanent relationship rather than transient emotions like those excited by a mundane performance. Other than this significant difference, there is great similarity between the workings of the *rasa* of loving Krishna and those of aesthetic theory: *rasa*, it is said, is awakened through a complex series of appropriate excitants (*vibhavas*), manifestations (*anubhavas*), and auxiliary feelings (*vyabhichari-bhavas*). When the *rasa* of *krishna-bhakti* is properly awakened, however, it will affect those who experience it in a way that no ordinary performance can. Bodily manifestations of devotional ecstasy (*sattvika-bhavas*), such as weeping and horripilation (hairs standing on end), will appear, transforming one into a lover of God.

DRAMA

"The Vaisnava dramas...have an importance that goes far beyond their undoubted function as recreation. They are complexly evolved, extensive in outreach, effective in communicating religious experience, and an important instrument of education in the society in which we find them."

— Norvin Hein
Professor Emeritus, Yale University

The Sanskrit *Natya-shastra*, compiled by the sage Bharata Muni, is considered among the world's earliest manuals on playwriting and dramaturgy. The work includes a story in which the demigods approach Lord Brahma, the creator, saying, "We desire entertainment, a form of artistic expression that uses visual, musical, narrative, and poetic devices in an uplifting way." In response, Brahma created drama. Describing his new creation, Brahma said, "Drama will become a source of instruction for the world."

In the *Natya-shastra*, Bharata Muni not only defines the laws governing ideal literary creation, but precisely delineates how each work of dramatic literature should be performed. He divides dramatic arts into four categories: *vachika*—the art of voice, intonation and speech delivery;

angika—movements, gestures, and poses of the body and limbs; *aharya* and *nepathyaga*—make-up and costumes, as well as stage props and decoration; and *sattvika*—the conforming of the actor's consciousness to the part he has to play and the emotions he has to convey.

The art of Sanskrit drama borrows technique and style from the Vedas: it takes recitation from the *Rig Veda*, song and melody from the *Sama Veda*, acting from the *Yajur Veda*, and sentiments and emotions from the *Atharva Veda*.

In the same way that *rasa* (literally, the "taste" one has for a particular relationship with the Divine) is an important religious concept in Vedic literature, "taste" or "mood" is the essence of Sanskrit dramatic theory. The traditional goal of a Vaishnava actor is to make the *rasa* of a play's dramatic meaning accessible to an audience and thus evoke emotions and heart-felt responses. The task of

the dramatist and the actors is to make the complexities of dramatic *rasa* felt by the audience, engulfing everyone in an experience that, though it may be instructive, is deep in its emotions.

Vaishnavas thus relish dramatic literature. It is felt that philosophy and theology are best expressed in poetry and plays. A single poem or dramatic performance is considered more likely to evoke religious feeling and understanding than thousands of pages of reasoned argument. Religious experience, like any experience, is inefficiently communicated by mere language. When the senses are engaged in viewing a dramatic performance, however, there is greater likelihood of being psychologically and emotionally transported into the reality that is re-created on the stage.

Consequently, Vaishnava authors have produced a great variety of plays. One of the earliest (circa 1st century C.E.) is the five-act *Balcharita*, attributed to Bhasa, which focuses on Krishna's childhood activities. Many centuries later the playwright Shesha Krishna composed a drama similar to *Balcharita*, named *Krishnakavi*. Such plays are still brought to life by the Ras-lila troupes of Braj, for example, who perform them annually.

Two early Gaudiya-Vaishnava dramas are Ramananda Roy's *Jagannath-vallabha-natakam* and Kavi Karnapur's *Chaitanya-chandrodaya-natakam* (both circa 16th century).

The former focuses on the love of Radha and Krishna, while the latter depicts the life of Shri Chaitanya. Rupa Goswami's *Vidagdha-madhava*, a play about Krishna's intimate pastimes in Vrindavan, as well as his *Lalita-madhava*, which focuses on Krishna's later life in Dvaraka, are perhaps the most revered plays in the Gaudiya-Vaishnava canon.

Shri Chaitanya Mahaprabhu Himself engaged in dramatic performances with His associates. His biographers call special attention to His role as Rukmini, Krishna's wife in Dvaraka. When Mahaprabhu would don the costume and makeup of Rukmini, He would virtually enter her reality. So authentic was His performance that Vaishnavas would forget He was only acting.

THE ULTIMATE DRAMA

For Rupa Goswami and other Vaishnava theologians, the only drama that can produce true *rasa*, or taste, is the divine play of Krishna, which is seen as the ultimate reality. David Haberman, associate professor of religious studies at Indiana University, writes, "The emphasis for Rupa is not on the ability of generic drama to lift one out of everyday experience; rather, he is deeply concerned with the means by which one may participate in the one Real Drama.... For the Gaudiya Vaishnava, salvation comes to be defined as an eternal participation in this absolute drama."

Dance

In the spiritual world, say Vaishnava poets, "every word is a song, every step a dance." Krishna dances on the heads of the Kaliya serpent, and He engages in the famous *rasa-lila* dance with the *gopis*. Indeed, the whole material creation is often thought of in terms of Shiva's cosmic dance. Responding to the divine dancing of God, devotees dance for Him as well.

In the 16th century, ecstatic dancing was an integral part of Shri Chaitanya's nocturnal *kirtans* (kirtan—glorifying the Lord with song and praise). Since then, a distinguishing characteristic of Gaudiya-Vaishnava *kirtan* has been impassioned dancing.

Temple dancers, such as the Devadasis in Puri, are considered elevated devotees, as immersed in God as the whirling dervishes of Sufism. Like all other components of the tradition, sacred Indian dance has developed into a complex art-form, involving *mudras* (hand gestures), *abhinayanas* (facial expressions and bodily movements), and *gati* (intricate footwork). There are four main traditions of Indian dance, each with its own unique style and technique: Bharata Natyam, which originated in the southern region of Tamil Nadu; Kathakali, traced to Kerala; Kathak, from the northern state of Uttar Pradesh; and Manipuri, unique to the state of Manipur. All of these forms of dance, as well as the many other types of classical and folk dances, are used in the Vaishnava tradition to depict the pastimes of Krishna and His multifarious incarnations.

Traditional Indian dance is both beautiful and thought-provoking. In general, it tells a story associated with the life of Krishna and other divine personalities. It is also an expression of exuberance, in which one celebrates one's devotion to God.

SEVERAL MUDRAS AND THEIR MEANINGS

Vishnu

Shiva

Woman

Peacock

Flower

Half Moon

Beautiful

Sorrowful

Music

"Music is the mediator between intellectual and sensuous life…the one spiritual entrance into the higher world."

—Ludwig van Beethoven

"Music praises God. Music is well or better able to praise Him than the building of a church with all its decoration; music is the church's greatest ornament."   —Igor Stravinsky

The joyous feelings awakened through music, hymns, and melodious glorification of God are a kind of sonic theology, in which both performer and audience can understand the Divine in ways difficult to apprehend through other means. This is apparent in Vaishnavism, where for millennia music has been an inseparable part of its mystical tradition.

Divinities are often musicians: The Goddess Sarasvati plays her *vina* (the Indian lute), the celestial sage Narada plays his—thus both celebrate their way through the material cosmos. Lord Krishna charms the universe with the mellifluous notes of His magical flute, and Lord Shiva dances the cosmic dance of destruction while playing on his *dindin* drum.

In North India, the rich field of Vaishnava music has given rise to several distinct styles, each marked by subtle yet definite differences.

The Gaudiya musical styles, such as Narottam das's Garan-hati, Shrinivas's Manohar Shahi, and Shyamananda's Reneti—all have distinguishing techniques. Garan-hati, for example, starts slowly and melodically, with a simple beat, gradually building up to greater complexity and finally a crescendo, with exuberant singing and dancing. As opposed to other forms of *kirtan*, this unique form of Vaishnava music always includes *Gaura-chandrika* lyrics (i.e., prayers to Shri Chaitanya that reveal His identity as Krishna) before praising Krishna directly.

Nonetheless, all forms of North Indian *kirtan* employ tonal and polytonal rhythms (*tala*), established melodic formats (*raga*), gestures of emotional expression (*abhinaya*), and dancing (*natyam*).

One finds an equally developed

musical tradition in the South. The technique called *araiyar* ("to speak," "to proclaim") is associated with singer-dancers from the most prominent Shrivaishnava temples. *Araiyar* employs complex vocal techniques, dancing styles, and, on certain holidays, dramatic performance. The *Divya Prabandham*, the much-revered mystical poetry of the Alvars, provides the basis for the countless musical styles of the South, including the *araiyar*.

South Indian Vaishnava music was developed by devotee-musicians, such as Purandara Das and Tyagaraj, who popularized Vaishnava music in Karnatak. The many forms of Vaishnava music are now being documented by the Madras Music Academy. The musicologists there have officially adopted the following as their slogan: *kanu bina gita nahi*, "Without Krishna, there is no song."

VAISHNAVA MUSICAL INSTRUMENTS

While any musical instrument can be incorporated into the various forms of Vaishnava music, the more commonly used instruments are as follows:

1. **Mridanga (Khol):** A double-sided drum made of clay. A similar instrument, the *pakhowaj*, is made of wood, distinguishing it from the traditional mridanga both in sound and in appearance.

2. **Kartals:** Hand cymbals, which allow the musicians to keep a beat and their audience to become almost hypnotically drawn into the music.

3. **Vishana (horn):** Horns are occasionally used during *kirtan* in a random fashion.

4. **Harmonium:** A keyboard instrument, in which the tones are produced by pumping air through metal reeds by means of steadily pushed bellows.

5. **Vina:** A lutelike instrument of the zither family, with seven strings along a pear-shaped fretted neck.

6. **Tanpura:** Commonly made of dried pumpkin or wood, the *tanpura* is a stringed instrument similar to a sitar, with four to six droning strings played one after the other, usually as background for other instruments.

"Who is the yogi? Who is the priest? Not just the privileged few may follow the path of yoga or make acceptable offerings in the temple. Everyone, men and women, high caste and low, may be a yogi of devotion or may offer the simple fruits of action to the Lord."

—Diana L. Eck
Department of Sanskrit and Indian Studies,
Harvard University

PRACTITIONERS 9

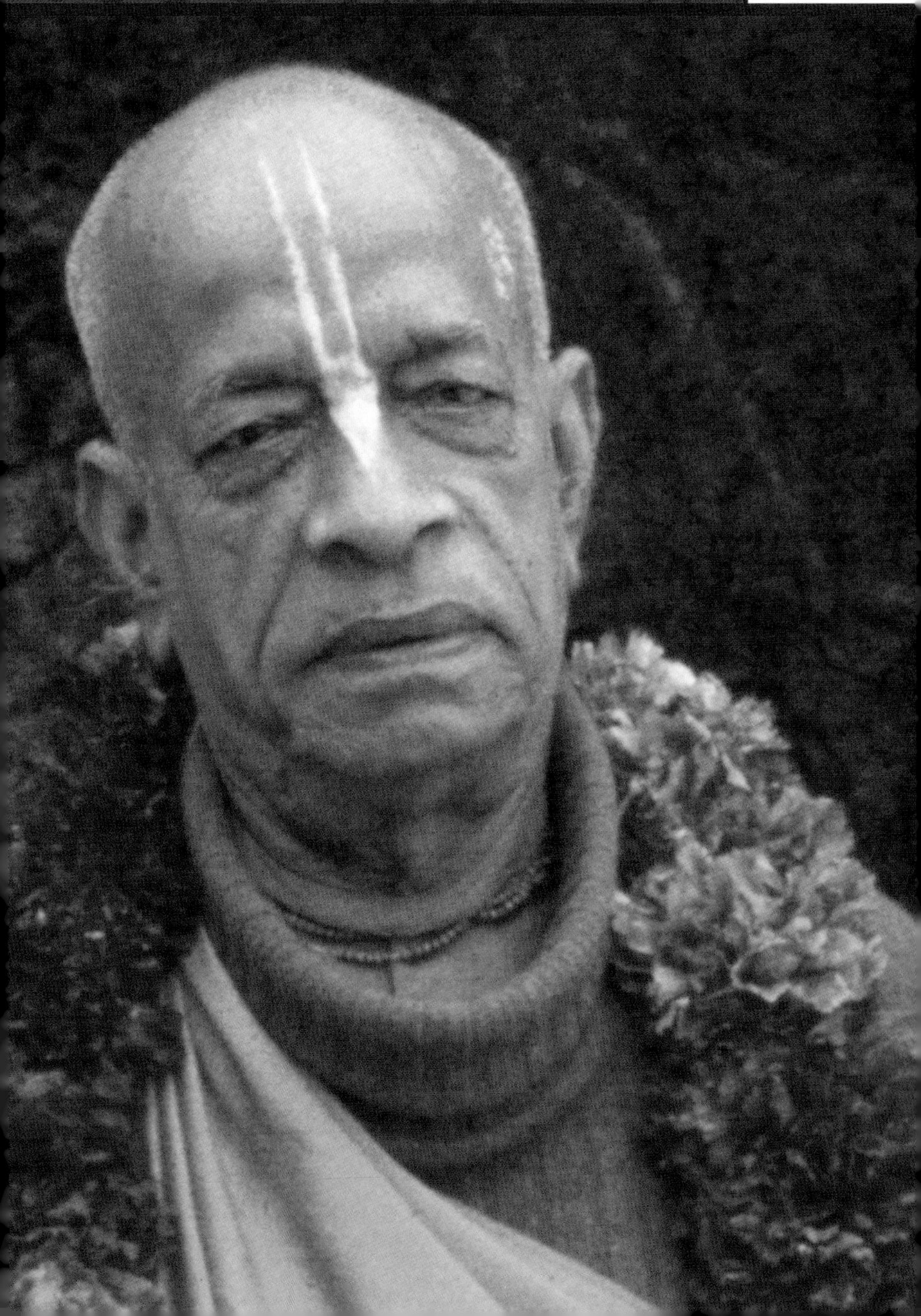

WHAT IS A? Devotee

One who engages in bhakti-yoga—loving devotional service to the Supreme (Krishna or Vishnu)—is known as a *bhakta* (a devotee), or a Vaishnava. In contrast to the paths of *karma-yoga* (which engages the body) and *gyana-yoga* (which engages the mind), the way of *bhakti* encompasses these two paths, engaging the heart as well. The Vaishnava scriptures say that if a person lives the life of a *bhakta*, in a previous lifetime he must already have achieved the perfection of all other methods of yoga.

According to the most liberal definition, to be a *bhakta* does not require even conscious awareness of a relationship with the Supreme. Every living thing by virtue of its simple existence as part and parcel of God is a *bhakta*. Thus, Vaishnava scriptures assert that every living soul is by constitution a servant of Krishna. By this definition, every living thing—plant, animal, and so on—is a devotee.

A more usual definition is found in the *Chaitanya-charitamrita*, where Lord Chaitanya Himself says, "Anyone who appreciates the chanting of the holy name of the Lord is

to be counted among the *bhaktas*." Here, a simple appreciation is required. Practitioners of other faiths—to the degree they are in touch with the essence of their tradition and appreciate glorification of God—are *bhaktas*. Such a nonsectarian definition of *bhakta* can also be seen in the comment of Bhaktivinode Thakur, the great Vaishnava teacher, who, upon entering a Christian church, remarked, "How nicely my Lord is being worshiped here."

The highest level of *bhakta*, in the most demanding sense of the term, is the pure devotee. One is considered a pure *bhakta* when spontaneous

love of God arises in his heart. Prior to this, the *bhakta* may engage in the practices of *bhakti* out of a sense of duty, but real loving service, the hallmark of true *bhakti*, may remain far away. Association with a pure *bhakta* brings one into association with Krishna.

THE Guru
PRINCIPLE

When people hear the words "guru," or "spiritual master," they might think of honorable teachers, exemplary people with whom they or their friends are familiar. It could be a priest, a rabbi, or the local yoga instructor.

The words might also conjure up images of opportunistic con men, controversial swamis who exploit others for personal comfort, wealth, and power. Exactly what is a guru, and what do the original sacred texts on the subject have to say about it? Let us begin by focusing on two primary issues. First the question of necessity: For spiritual matters, does one need a guru? Second: Just how can you tell whether a person who claims to be a guru is genuine?

The controversy can be resolved when one centers on two primary issues. First, the question of necessity: Does one need a teacher for spiritual matters? The second question involves a guru's qualifications: Just what makes a person a genuine guru?

The Vedic scriptures assert that just as a teacher is required in any area of knowledge, the same holds true for spiritual education. Saint

Thomas Aquinas, although known to possess a deeply analytical and philosophical mind, nevertheless studied under Albertus Magnus. Aristotle accepted Plato as his teacher, and Plato studied under Socrates. When Krishna came to this world, He accepted Sandipani Muni as His spiritual preceptor. Chaitanya Mahaprabhu accepted Ishvara Puri. The point is clear: regardless of one's spiritual qualifications, one still requires a spiritual teacher. As the scriptures state, "To learn transcendental science, one *must* approach a bona fide spiritual master [guru] in discipedic succession [*shrotriyam*]. The bona fide spiritual master is fixed in the Absolute Truth [*brahma-nishtham*]." (*Mundaka Upanishad* 1.2.12)

This verse not only emphasizes the importance of accepting a spiritual master but begins to address our second question: What are the qualifications of a bona fide guru? The word *shrotriyam* indicates that a guru must come in a historical succession of teachers, also known as a *sampradaya* ("lineage"). The Puranas speak of four such genuine lineages: the Shri-sampradaya, the Rudra-sampradaya, the Kumara-sampradaya, and the Brahma-sampradaya. The Puranas also mention the four prominent systematizers of these *sampradayas:* Ramanuja, Vishnusvami, Nimbarka, and Madhva. A Vaishnava guru should come in one of these four lineages.

In addition, the essence of the knowledge taught by the guru must be in accordance with *shastra* (the sacred texts) and *sadhus* (the other truly saintly persons throughout history). The guru must also be "fixed in transcendence" (*brahma-nishtham*), having traversed the path of spiritual illumination; this, again, should be confirmed by spiritual authorities in a disciplic succession and by the scriptures.

Vaishnava texts describe three types of guru: the *diksha-guru*, the shiksha-guru, and the *chaitya-guru.* The first two offer spiritual light from the outside, while the third, the Lord in the heart, lights the way from within. The *diksha-guru* serves the function of "initiating" one into transcendental knowledge. The serious student is given a new name, indicating his spiritual affiliation with a *sampradaya*. The *diksha-guru* also gives the student a sacred formula, or mantra, on which to meditate. The *shiksha-guru* functions as an instructor who expounds upon the teachings received from the *diksha-guru*. The *shiksha-guru* can be one or many, but the *diksha-guru* is never more than one.

The *chaitya-guru*—God Himself, within one's heart—enables the sincere aspirant to understand the esoteric significance of the transcendental themes and teachings received from the *diksha-* and *shiksha-gurus*.

The guru gives the spiritual seeker a new birth. This is a spiritual birth, in which divine knowledge and realization (*divya-gyana*) arise in the heart. By chanting the mantra received from the guru, one gradually gains knowledge of one's self, of the Lord, and of one's own relationship with the Lord.

The scriptures say that the guru is worthy of the highest honor but if he or she fails to meet the major scriptural requirements for a spiritual guide, such a person should be abandoned. However, if the spiritual master is genuine—having all the above qualities as well as *shrotriyam* and *brahma-nishtham*—he or she is an indispensable mediator between the devotee and the Lord.

SHRILA PRABHUPADA

A MODERN-DAY MASTER

His Divine Grace A. C. Bhaktivedanta Swami Prabhupada began the International Society for Krishna Consciousness (ISKCON) in New York City in 1966. He came to the West as a representative of the Brahma-Madhva-Gaudiya Sampradaya—a lineage dating back to antiquity.

Shrila Prabhupada was born of devoted Gaudiya Vaishnava parents in Calcutta, India, in 1896. His father's name was Gour Mohan De and his mother's, Rajani. He was named Abhay Charan, but sometimes he was called Nandu because he was born on Nandotsava—the day immediately following Krishna's birthday celebration. Shrila Prabhupada's early childhood was steeped in Krishna culture. From his earliest days he was extremely fond of Lord Krishna and Ratha-yatra, and he would regularly stage his own miniature Ratha-yatra festivals. Although he preferred to play his small *mridanga* (clay drum) rather than attend school, his mother's counsel prevailed, and Abhay Charan excelled in his studies, taking particular interest in oral expression, debate, and discussion. He completed his higher education in philosophy, economics, and English at Calcutta's Scottish Churches' College, and shortly thereafter became dedicated to the cause of Mahatma Gandhi. While a young nationalist, he started a family and developed a successful pharmaceutical concern.

All this was to change, however, in 1922, when he met his soon-to-be guru, Shrila Bhaktisiddhanta Sarasvati Thakur. Bhaktisiddhanta Sarasvati was one of the great Vaishnava renunciants of modern India, a singularly gifted scholar who translated complex philosophical texts and successfully established Gaudiya-Vaishnava monasteries throughout the subcontinent. He

was Prabhupada's link with the Brahma-Madhva-Gaudiya Sampradaya. Both pure and learned, he had a deep effect on Prabhupada. Within ten years he not only initiated Prabhupada as a disciple but gave him a life mission: to explain the universal message of Shri Chaitanya Mahaprabhu in the English language and to help the world with this knowledge.

Shrila Prabhupada began by publishing articles, and in 1944 started a magazine, *Back to Godhead*. In 1959 he took *sannyasa* (the renounced order of life). After this, Prabhupada dedicated his life to fulfilling the order of his spiritual master.

In 1965, at age sixty-nine, alone and with only forty rupees in his possession, His Divine Grace set sail from Calcutta. His destination: America. He carried within himself an intense desire to bring the balm of God consciousness to a materialistic world. It was with this hope and intent that he founded ISKCON, the International Society for Krishna Consciousness. In the decade that followed, Prabhupada established 108 temples in major cities around the world and initiated thousands of spiritual seekers of all races and ages. In addition, he established farm communities, founded religious elementary schools, and opened vegetarian restaurants.

Many revere Shrila Prabhupada as India's greatest scholar, philosopher, prophet, and cultural ambassador. According to the 1976 *Britannica Book of the Year*, he "astonished academic and literary communities worldwide by writing and publishing fifty-two

books on the ancient Vedic culture… in the period from October 1968 to November 1975."

Prabhupada's books, now translated into more than eighty languages, are being used in many of North America's universities and in thousands of libraries throughout the world. His *Back to Godhead* magazine continues as a bi-monthly after almost sixty years of publication.

What Prabhupada achieved in twelve years is legendary. He left this world in 1977 in Vrindavan (the holy land most dear to Lord Krishna), having circled the globe fourteen times—writing books, translating scriptures, giving lectures, and personally guiding his disciples all the while.

SADHUS

In India, Vaishnava and Shaivite monks meditate in the jungles or share their wealth of knowledge in the cities, their **distinct dress** and religious demeanor marking them as serious followers of a renounced way of life. Shakta, Buddhist, and Jain mendicants go door to door begging alms. Yogis and meditators can be found sitting by trees or holy rivers and concentrating on divine forms and **sacred mantras**. All of these deeply religious figures are sadhus—an integral part of India's landscape.

A sadhu is a renunciant, an individual who has set aside worldly goals and aspirations, focusing instead on spiritual ones. He has renounced this world in favor of the next. Many *sadhus* are *sannyasis* (members of the renounced order of life), although the definition is not limited to this order alone. Householders and others can be considered *sadhus* if their primary concern is the religious pursuit. The appellation of *sadhu* was originally given to those adept in *sadhana* ("spiritual practice"). Thus the word *sadhu* was derived.

Mention should also be made of a class of individuals who, for personal power and profit or due to lack of knowledge, feign spiritual advancement or invent spiritual practices not authorized by scriptures. Vaishnavas refer to such persons as *sahajiyas*—a word that has come to mean "imitationist" but originally referred to certain offshoot (heterodox) Buddhist and Vaishnava sects.

Sadhus are a diverse lot, and only scriptural study can distinguish the saints from the swindlers.

Women

The Indian mindset is generally viewed as supporting patriarchy in religious, economic, and social contexts. However, the earliest Vedic texts impressively emphasized the deep respect to be accorded to women. Indeed, the Vedas tell us, "Where women are honored, the demigods rejoice." Thus, women were to be valued for their contribution to family and society, and they were seen as being goddesses of the household. Yet in some respects the early traditions were conservative, declaring that women are always to be dependent on (and thus protected by) men—whether her father, husband, or eldest son. While Indian tradition respectfully regards all women as "mother," it equally views them as temptresses, with the power to divert men from their spiritual goals.

The overriding view of women in Vedic tradition, however, is one of deep respect. The *Bhagavad-gita* associates the feminine gender with finer qualities, such as wisdom, for Krishna states, "Among women, I am fame, fortune, fine speech, memory, intelligence, steadfastness, and patience."

When the *bhakti* (devotional) movement, which emphasized salvation for all, swept the subcontinent in the 16th century,

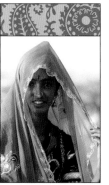

it became even more obvious how women might partake of these qualities. Several prominent figures in the *bhakti* movement were women; this provided new role models for Indian women. Bahinabai, a spiritually elevated Maharashtrian Vaishnavi, tolerated an abusive marriage, but ultimately reformed her husband to a religious way of life. Mirabai's approach to *stridharma*, or "womanly devotion," was quite the opposite of Bahinabai's.

She saw only Krishna as her husband, and her poetry reflected this single-minded devotion. Antal Alvar, one of the most significant saints of South India, was a female *bhakta* who composed ecstatic spiritual poetry that is revered and recited by Shrivaishnavas to this day.

These women and many others serve as powerful religious role models, their example encouraging Vaishnava women to develop their finer qualities in service to God. They are recognized for their spiritual virtues by all sectors of the Vaishnava world.

Perhaps the most significant example of a woman who excelled in Vaishnava dharma is Jahnava Devi. Here was an exemplary female devotee who became a leader among the Vaishnavas of late 16th-century Bengal. So respected was she that the most prominent devotees of the time, such as Narottam Das Thakur and Shrinivas Acharya, bowed down to her, rendering service and inquiring from her in a spirit of submission. She was held in extreme honor and reverence—and still is—by all Gaudiya Vaishnavas.

Jesus in india?

With his emphasis on love and his disregard for social stratification, Jesus preached a doctrine similar to that of the bhakti movements of India. In fact, the content and mood of his message are so close to those of Vaishnava *bhakti* that many conclude there may have been direct contact between Jesus and India.

Ancient Pali manuscripts talk about a "Saint Issa." According to some, this is a reference to Jesus, mentioning his sojourn in the land of the Ganges. Early European and Russian travelers unearthed similar documents attesting to Jesus's journey East. Writers as diverse as Reverend C. R. Potter and Edgar Cayce, both writing from a Christian perspective, and Andreas Faber-Kaiser, writing from a Muslim point of view, assert that Jesus went to India in the missing eighteen years of his life, or after his crucifixion, or both. (The Bible tells of Jesus's activities from birth to age twelve, and then of his three-year ministry after age thirty; his thirteenth through thirtieth years remain unaccounted for.) To date, no one can state with any certainty whether or not the stories of Jesus's sojourn in India are true.

While Western theologians remain divided about Jesus's visit to the Orient, the Vaishnava scripture *Bhavishya Purana* (nonsectarian in its scope) foretells Jesus's journey to India: A wandering ascetic is asked by a notable Maharaj, Shalewahin

by name, to identify himself. The ascetic answers that his name is Issa (the Indic form of Jesus), that he is the Son of God, the expected Messiah of his people, and that he was born

Pali texts indicate that Jesus may have visited these regions

Kabul

Leh

Lhasa

Kapilavastu

Benares

Rajabhita

Puri

of a virgin. He also mentions the Amalekites, an ancient tribe directly related to the biblical tradition. Thus, the *Bhavishya Purana* predicts Jesus's appearance, and many Vaishnavas consequently accept Jesus as the Son of God, for this is how he identifies himself in both the Bible and the Puranas. Krishna is seen as God, Jesus's Father. Krishna declares of Himself: "I am the father of the universe, the mother, the support, and the grandsire." (*Bg.* 9.17) Who can say that when Jesus prays "Our father who art in heaven…" it is not Krishna to whom he is praying?

"By constant endeavor for self-realization with the help of scriptural evidence, theistic conduct, and perseverance in practice, one can attain the highest devotion."
—*Brahma-samhita* 5.59

Varnashrama
The Vedic Social System

Vedic culture takes into account the psychophysical nature of individuals through a system called Varnashrama Dharma. Unfortunately, this system has often been misidentified as the caste system. In the caste system, people are classified according to birth: if one is born into a *brahmana* (priestly, or intellectual) family, for example, one is automatically considered a *brahmana*, despite one's qualifications or lack thereof. Clearly, this has been the cause of much unrest and civil strife in modern India.

The true Varnashrama system emphasizes "quality and work," not birth: one is fit for a particular occupation according to one's qualifications, not according to the family into which one was born.

This system is delineated in the *Bhagavad-gita* (4.13), where it is described as the foundation of a properly functioning society. The Varnashrama system is comprised of four basic *varnas* (groups according to material occupations or duties): (1) *brahmanas* (intellectuals and priests), (2) *kshatriyas* (administrators and military people), (3) *vaishyas* (farmers and business people), and (4) *shudras* (manual laborers). Any given individual may fit in a combination of these categories, but one occupational inclination will predominate.

There are likewise four spiritual stages (*ashramas*) in the Varnashrama system: (1) *brahmacharya* (celibate student life), (2) *grihastha* (married life), (3) *vanaprastha* (retired life), and (4) *sannyasa* (renunciation and complete dedication to the Absolute). Each *varna* and *ashrama* is governed by a different set of rules. An understanding of the original Varnashrama system (and not the later caste system) is a prerequisite for understanding the Vaishnava social outlook, which emphasizes Daivi ("Divine") Varnashrama—that is to say, the standard Varnashrama system, but specifically directed toward the Supreme.

A brahmachari *studies until the age of twenty-five, at which time he may marry and live as a* grihastha. *As old age approaches, he may retire and take* sannyasa, *renouncing worldly ties.*

*A representation of the social body—*brahmanas *represent the head of society,* kshatriyas *the upper body,* vaishyas *the lower body, and* shudras *the legs. This conception, which traces back to the Rig Veda, is echoed in Plato's* Republic, *where he argues that social classes correspond to a hierarchy of personality types. The class pre-dominated by the philosophical intellect, he says, is the highest; after that come those dominated by the emotions; and finally we find those in whom the "appetites" (sensual desires) predominate. Further, says Plato, one finds that society is divided in a similar way. On top are the philosopher-kings, who rule; below them are the warriors; and finally, we have the merchants and workers, whom Plato merges into one category.*

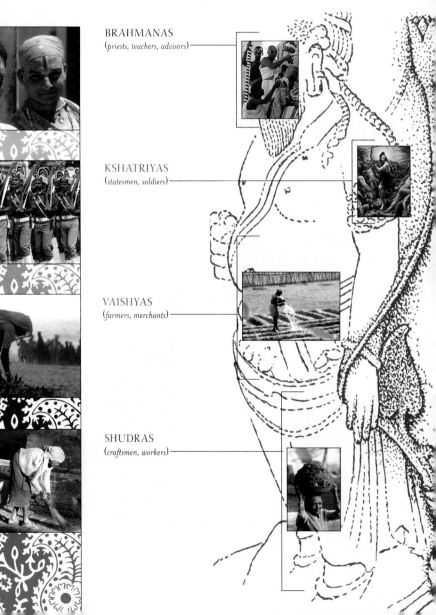

BRAHMANAS
(priests, teachers, advisors)

KSHATRIYAS
(statesmen, soldiers)

VAISHYAS
(farmers, merchants)

SHUDRAS
(craftsmen, workers)

Yoga

When a Westerner thinks of traditional India, some form of **yoga** or meditation comes to mind. Because the yoga system is described in eight steps (see chart on page 156), it is sometimes called **ashtanga-yoga**, "the eightfold path," but it is more commonly known as **hatha-yoga**. The word "yoga" comes from the Sanskrit root *yuj*, which means "to link up with, to combine." It is similar to *religio*, the Latin root of the word "religion," which means "to bind together." Religion and yoga, then, have the same end in mind: combining or linking with God.

Yoga was systematized in medieval India by Patanjali in his *Yoga-sutras*, a text that explains the methodical process whereby one can learn to control the body and mind, with the ultimate goal of using these finely tuned material instruments in the service of the Lord. In yoga the body is viewed as the temple of the soul. By means of postures (*asanas*) and breath control (*pranayama*), yoga promotes physical health and mental well-being that help strengthen the "temple." In the West, the physical fitness part of it has become an end in itself. According to the traditional yoga system, however, this was merely the first step on the path of God realization.

Just as we in the West may overlook the deep spiritual foundation of yoga, Indian yogic adepts can be distracted from the ultimate goal to the attainment of *siddhis*, or "mystic perfections." These are described in chapter three of Patanjali's *Yoga-sutras*. There are eight kinds of mystic yogic perfections, among which are the ability to assume a minute size (*anima-siddhi*), the ability to float in air or on water (*laghima-siddhi*), and the power to immediately acquire things from far-off distances (*prapti-siddhi*).

All of the *yoga-siddhis* are ultimately material achievements, as attainable through materialist science as through yoga. For example,

laghima-siddhi, the ability to float in air or on water, is also possible by means of airplane or boat. *Vashita-siddhi*, which enables one to bring someone under control, can also be achieved through hypnosis.

Unlike these yogic perfections, the aim of *bhakti-yoga* is to enhance one's relationship with the Supreme—an outcome that has no material counterpart. In the sixth chapter of *Bhagavad-gita*, Krishna in effect tells Arjuna not to worry, for he, Arjuna, is already the best of yogis. Krishna tells him that of all yogis—including *hatha-yogis, gyana-yogis, dhyana-yogis, karma-yogis,* and *bhakti-yogis*—the best is the *bhakti-yogi*: "Of all yogis, the one with great faith who always abides in Me, thinks of Me within himself, and renders transcendental loving service to Me—he is the most intimately united with Me in yoga and is the highest of all."

THE YOGA SYSTEM

THE 8 STEPS OF ASHTANGA-YOGA

Remote Preparation

1. *yama* (practice of precepts)
   - *ahimsa* (nonviolence)
   - *satya* (truthfulness)
   - *asteya* (nonstealing)
   - *brahmacharya* (continence)
   - *apavigraha* (absence of greed)

2. *niyama* (practice of virtues)
   - *saucha* (purity)
   - *santosha* (peacefulness)
   - *tapas* (discipline)
   - *svadhyaya* (study, especially of sacred texts)
   - *ishvara pranidhana* (surrender to God)

3. *asana* (postures)
4. *pranayama* (breath control)
5. *pratyahara* (withdrawal of the senses)

Direct Preparation

6. *dharana* (concentration)
7. *dhyana* (meditation)
8. *samadhi* (trance)

Advanced Practice

The exercise of extraordinary powers and the practice of advanced forms of meditation, leading to *kaivalya* (complete absorption and freedom).

"… and when the yogi engages himself with sincere endeavor in making further progress, being washed of all contaminations, then ultimately, achieving perfection after many, many births of practice, he attains the supreme goal."

—Lord Krishna
Bhagavad-gita 6.45

MEDITATION

"What was obtained in the Satya Age by meditation on Vishnu, in the Treta Age by elaborate sacrifice, in the Dvapara Age by image worship, comes in the Kali Age through chanting the name of Krishna."

— *Shrimad Bhagavatam* 12.3.52

Meditation is a natural component of yoga. Traditional yogic systems employ complex meditation techniques as frequently as sitting postures, since both are useful in developing a sound body and mind. To quiet the mind and provide a point of focus, the spiritual aspirant concentrates upon mantras, ranging from Sanskrit syllables to names of God. Vaishnava texts recommend the names of God as particularly effective in the current age. In the Vaishnava system of meditation, three distinct forms are *japa, kirtan,* and *sankirtan.* In *japa* the meditator softly recites to himself God's name with the use of a rosary (japa-mala) of 108 beads. *Kirtan*, on the other hand, is a "public meditation," in which one loudly sings the name of God, often accompanied by musical instruments and dancing. When performed in a group, with other worshipers, this is called *sankirtan.*

In the meditational technique known as lila-smaranam ("pastime remembrance"), the aspirant chiefly focuses on the names (*nama*), form (*rupa*), qualities (*guna*), and pastimes (*lila*) of Krishna. The practitioner begins such meditation on Krishna by chanting His holy name in a regulated way, under the guidance of a spiritual master. The beginner generally has little ability to concentrate, yet due to study of scripture and a sincerity of purpose, even at this early stage one acquires a memory (*smaranam*) of Krishna. With the inner longing to gain focus, the ability to concentrate (*dharana*) develops. The enhanced familiarity with *krishna-lila* leads to the next level, in which

the practitioner learns to meditate in a more direct way (*dhyana*), gradually developing expertise in visualizing the pastimes of the Lord. Becoming accomplished in this art, he learns to meditate without interference (*dhruvanusmriti*), and throughout the day can focus on the object of meditation without substantial distraction. The final stage entails complete absorption (*samadhi*), wherein one comes face to face with the Deity and is situated in a separate reality.

The meditating yogi raises his consciousness through the various chakras, or energy centers, of the body. These begin with the muladhara ("root") chakra, and elevate through the chakras of earth, water, fire, air, sound, light, and thought (as depicted on the yogi's body). By raising the life energy to the topmost chakra, one reaches perfection. However, the devotee of Vishnu, through chanting, opens these same chakras in a more direct way, quickly enabling the journey back to Godhead.

Mandalas & Yantras

Mandalas are visual diagrams that, when meditated upon, unlock esoteric mysteries. They can be fashioned out of wood or bronze like a sculpture, painted on cloth or paper, or drawn on the ground with colorful dyes or threads. *Mandala* is the Sanskrit word for "circle," and, indeed, *mandalas* are usually circular formations, representing "sacred space" or a "microcosm of reality." In the center of the *mandala* is generally a *bindu*, a small dot, which represents the center of the universe. The goal for one who meditates on the *mandala* is to travel to the center, thereby reaching enlightenment. *Mandalas* are often composed of intricate mazes of triangles and squares, which makes the journey to the center difficult.

The psychologist Carl Jung (1875–1961) wrote extensively about *mandalas*. The subject became interesting to him when a good number of his patients, for no apparent reason, had vivid dreams of geometric shapes and as a result were inclined to draw *mandala*-like formations. After several trips to India, Jung concluded that *mandalas* exist in the "collective unconscious" of humanity. He viewed the ancient Vedic texts that first brought these forms to light as a significant area of study, demanding further research.

Mandalas are commonly used by yogis and impersonalists, as opposed to Vaishnavas. Those who reach perfection in this form of meditation seek to internalize the cosmos upon which they focus, and merge with it.

However, there are also Vaishnava *mandalas*, and these are shapes and forms that represent Krishna and His inner circle of devotees. The goal of this meditation is to enter into Krishna's *lila* in the spiritual world. Common examples are depictions of Braj-mandala, or the sacred area of Vrindavan where Krishna engages in His unlimited spiritual pastimes, and Rasa-mandala, the area where He engages in His *rasa* dance with the *gopis*.

When a mandala is considered a visual expression of a *mantra*—a holy sound that one can see—it is called a *yantra*. *Yantras* are generally used in tantricism, the process by which one attains liberation and bliss through the worship of the Goddess. The diagrams consist of exceedingly complex geometric patterns of overlapping triangles, squares, and circles. Monosyllabic mantras are inscribed on different parts of the *yantra*, thus making up together the "word-body" of the Goddess. The *bindu*, or dot, in the center represents the very essence of the deity. There are specific Vaishnava *yantras* in which Lakshmi, the wife of Vishnu, is meditated upon as the supreme goddess of the universe. There is also a *yantra* in which Radha-Krishna occupy the center of a lotus; the *gopis*, Their most intimate devotees, surround Them in the innermost ring of petals.

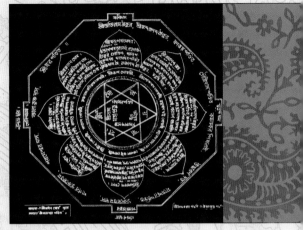

The goal of *yantra* meditation is to enable the practitioners to understand the Deity in relation to themselves, and to come to appreciate the Deity as the center of all things.

The mandala diagram above represents the spiritual Navadvip, or the abode of Shri Chaitanya.

The mandala to the left represents Shri Rama.

IDOLS AND DEITIES
THE DISTINCTION

Vaishnavism, like most religious traditions, views God as having both **transcendental** and immanent aspects to His nature. The Lord exists in His spiritual abode (transcendence) and is likewise present in the hearts of all individuals (immanence). Another aspect of God's immanence, and one that is unique to Vaishnavism, is the form of the Deity (*murti*). God becomes manifest not only in incarnations but in images. Thus, Vaishnavism sees the Deity as the "iconic incarnation" of the Lord.

During the colonization of India, the British, steeped in the Judeo-Christian tradition, found Deity worship peculiar and even abhorrent. Indeed, they referred to Lord Jagannath as "that Indian Moloch," seeing Him as a "graven image" or an "idol," against which there were clear taboos in the Bible.

The Vedic literature itself maintains a sharp distinction between idol and Deity. As Harvard scholar Diana Eck has written in *Darshan: Seeing the Divine Image in India*:

"Just as the term icon conveys the sense of a 'likeness,' so do the Sanskrit words pratikriti and pratima suggest the 'likeness' of the image to the deity it represents. The common word for such images, however, is murti, which is defined in Sanskrit as 'anything which has definite shape and limits,' 'a form, body, figure,' 'an embodiment, incarnation, manifestation.' Thus, the murti is more than a likeness; it is the deity itself taken 'form.'...The uses of the word murti in the Upanishads and the 'Bhagavad-gita' suggest that the form is its essence. The flame is the murti of fire, [etc.]..."

The Sanskrit texts called *Shilpa-shastras* give exact prescriptions for the fashioning of Deities. There are specifications for the proper stance of the Deities, their hand gestures, bodily proportions, etc., so that the "image" is not merely a function of the "imagination" of the artist. Trained in scriptural specifications for divine forms, the *shilpins* (as the artists who create the images are called) enter into moods of deep yogic meditation, thus fashioning images not

Deities of Krishna and His immediate expansion, Balaram.

In India, cows are venerated (see below) but not worshiped as God. The biblical tradition refers to "the golden calf" as the emblem of idolatry, and frowns upon such worship. In the Vaishnava tradition, idolatry is also frowned upon. But Deity worship, wherein forms of Krishna and His direct incarnations are revered, is an established part of Vaishnavism.

in accordance with fancy but in accordance with scriptural canon. After this, an elaborate ceremony is performed wherein the Lord is asked to "imbue the Deity with His divine presence." It is at this point that the Deity is ready to be worshiped and is placed in the temple. Worshipers can then come and have darshan ("seeing")—they see the Deity and the Deity sees them.

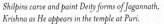

Shilpins carve and paint Deity forms of Jagannath, Krishna as He appears in the temple at Puri.

Deity WORSHIP

Ultimately, the image incarnation of the Lord is a divine "descent" by which the Lord entrusts Himself to human caretaking. The Deity is a divine guest and He must be treated as such. Therefore He is offered incense, flowers, lights, hymns, food—all of this is pleasing not only to the devotee's senses but also to the Deity's.

Moreover, this interaction establishes a loving exchange between the devotee and God.

"[Vaishnava] worship," Eck writes, "...is certainly not an occasion for yogic withdrawing of the senses... but it is rather an occasion for awakening the senses and directing them toward the divine. Entering the temple, a worshiper clangs a big overhead bell. The energy of the senses is harnessed to the apprehension of God. Thus, it is not only vision that is refined by *darshan*, but the other senses as well are focused, ever more sharply, on God."

As Eck says, "The image, which may be seen, bathed, adorned, touched, and honored, does not stand *between* the worshiper and the Lord, somehow receiving the honor properly due to the Supreme Lord. Rather, because the image is a form of the Supreme Lord, it is precisely the image that facilitates and enhances the close relationship of the worshiper and God and makes possible the deepest outpouring of emotions in worship."

It may be said that God's willingness to incarnate in the Deity form constitutes the ultimate expression of His love for humanity. This was beautifully expressed by Pillai Lokacharya, a great teacher in the Ramanujite tradition:

THE HIDDEN GLORY OF INDIA

"This is the greatest grace of the Lord, that being free He becomes bound, being independent He becomes dependent for all His service on the devotee.... In other forms, man belonged to God. But behold the supreme sacrifice of Ishvara [Krishna] in the form of the murti, for here the Almighty becomes the property of the devotee.... He carries the Lord about, fans Him, feeds Him, plays with Him—yea, the Infinite has become finite, that the child soul may grasp, understand, and love Him."

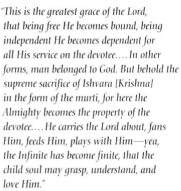

Language

Because India is culturally diverse, she is a reservoir of languages and dialects. The Constitution of India today recognizes eighteen major Indic languages. The latest census acknowledges 1,600 minor languages and dialects as well. Of all the languages of India, especially important for Vaishnavas are Hindi, Bengali, Tamil, Oriya, Kannada, and Sanskrit.

The languages of India are divided into two major groups: the Indo-Aryan languages (such as Hindi) in the north, and the Dravidian languages (such as Tamil, Telugu, and Kannada), native to the south. Sanskrit, the earliest of the Indo-Aryan languages, is believed to be the basis of many Indo-European languages, such as Greek and Latin, the Romance, Germanic, and Balto-Slavic languages, and many languages from Iran and the Middle East.

Sanskrit is considered the ancient tongue of seers and sages. According to Thomas J. Hopkins, professor of religion at Franklin and Marshall College in Pennsylvania, "Sanskrit words were not just arbitrary labels assigned to phenomena; they were the sound forms of objects, actions, and attributes, related to the corresponding reality in the same way as visual forms and different only in being perceived by the ear and not by the eye." Sanskrit is therefore called Devanagari (*deva*–"god," *nagari*–"city")—the language of the spiritual sphere.

Sanskrit (literally "polished," "refined," "perfected") is widely considered one of the oldest languages in the world. It is known to have gone through several stages of development. In its oldest form it is the language of the Vedic hymns, particularly the *Rig Veda*. Classical Sanskrit, which followed, was codified by the grammarian Panini around 500 B.C.E. Most of the Puranas and epics conform to Panini's rules. Even as the language developed

	DEVANAGARI	BENGALI	ORIYA		DEVANAGARI	BENGALI	ORIYA
ā	अ	অ	ଅ	ja	ज	জ	ଜ
ā	आ	আ	ଆ	jña	ज्ञ	জ্ঞ	ଜ୍ଞ
kā	का	কা	କା	ña	ञ	ঞ	ଞ
i	इ	ই	ଇ	ṭa	ट	ট	ଟ
ki	कि	কি	କି	ṭha	ठ	ঠ	ଠ
ī	ई	ঈ	ଈ	ḍa	ड	ড	ଡ
kī	की	কী	କୀ	ḍha	ढ	ঢ	ଢ
u	उ	উ	ଉ	ṇa	ण	ণ	ଣ
ku	कु	কু	କୁ	ta	त	ত	ତ
ū	ऊ	ঊ	ଊ	tha	थ	থ	ଥ
kū	कू	কূ	କୂ	da	द	দ	ଦ
ṛ	ऋ	ঋ	ଋ	dha	ध	ধ	ଧ
kṛ	कृ	কৃ	କୃ	na	न	ন	ନ
ē	ए	এ	ଏ	pa	प	প	ପ
kē	के	কে	କେ	pha	फ	ফ	ଫ
ai	ऐ	ঐ	ଐ	ba	ब	ব	ବ
kai	कै	কৈ	କୈ	bha	भ	ভ	ଭ
ō	ओ	ও	ଓ	ma	म	ম	ମ
kō	को	কো	କୋ	ya	य	য	ଯ
au	औ	ঔ	ଔ	ra	र	র	ର
kau	कौ	কৌ	କୌ	la	ल	ল	ଲ
ka	क	ক	କ	va	व	ব	ଵ
kha	ख	খ	ଖ	ça	श	শ	ଶ
ga	ग	গ	ଗ	ṣa	ष	ষ	ଷ
gha	घ	ঘ	ଘ	sa	स	স	ସ
ṅa	ङ	ঙ	ଙ	ha	ह	হ	ହ
ca	च	চ	ଚ	ṛa	ड़	ড়	ଡ଼
cha	छ	ছ	ଛ				

The three South Asian scripts Devanagari, Bengali, and Oriya are those most often used in the writing of Gaudiya Vaishnava literature. The Devanagari script is also used in Hindi.

into regional vernaculars, the earlier forms of Sanskrit remained the language of the learned and priestly classes. However, most of India's sacred texts, originally written in Sanskrit, were eventually translated into regional languages. This allowed them to reach a much wider audience. For example, the Hindi re-creation of the Sanskrit *Ramayana* (known as the *Ramcharitmanas*)—not a translation but a retelling—is known and loved in much of India. So too are translations and re-creations of other Puranas and epics into Gujarati, Bengali, Hindi, and so on.

DRESS

In India, like everywhere, clothing fucntions as an important marker of social classification. People communicate their identity and beliefs through the wearing of particular clothes, with various regional nuances of style. In general, the traditional dress for both men and women consists of various cloths elegantly draped over the body and held together by folds and tucks. In place of trousers (which, with modernity, are becoming more common) men wear the traditional dhoti (a loosely draped waistcloth) and a kurta (a long, loose-fitting shirt). The way in which the dhoti is folded on the body will reveal whether a man is a *sannyasi* (renunciant), a *brahmachari* (celibate student), or a *grihasta* (householder).

The sari, a single length of draped cloth, is still the most popular form of dress for women. Different draping methods reveal the part of the country from which one comes.

The color of one's dress is a clear indicator of social status. *Sannyasis* and *brahmacharis* wear saffron (representing celibacy), whereas householders (married men) wear white. White is also the color of dress for women who are widowed, in contrast to the bright colors and patterns of married women's saris.

Vaishnavas also wear various kinds of neck-beads, not merely for ornamental purposes but as an indication of religious commitment. A three-strand necklace of *tulasi* beads, for example, indicates that one has accepted a spiritual teacher (guru).

In addition to these sartorial components, hairstyle and bodily markings are also employed as indicators of religious affiliation. Vaishnava monks generally have shaven heads, keeping only a tuft of hair on the back of the head. This distinguishes them from Buddhists and the followers of Shankara, whose heads are completely shaven.

A woman will be viewed as either a prostitute or a respectable person depending upon the manner in which she parts her hair. Forehead markings are another essential element of identification in Vaishnava culture. Married women wear a *bindi*—a red dot in the center of the forehead. Today many young girls and unmarried women wear similar *bindis* in many colors, but these have no religious or social meaning.

Various styles of tilak (above) and traditional dress (right).

The markings called *tilak*, or *tika*, are applied with sacred clay or *chandan* (sandalwood paste) in various styles that distinguish followers of one *sampradaya* (spiritual lineage) from another. Worshipers of Shiva wear on their foreheads *tripundra*—three horizontal lines, while Vaishnavas wear *urdhvapundra*—two vertical lines often with a leaflike shape at the bottom (see chart).

The *Skanda Purana* states that the "U"-shape (the vertical lines) of the *urdhvapundra* represents the footprint of Krishna, and that the small triangular-shaped image at its base is a *tulasi* leaf, always found at Krishna's feet. Additionally, the *Padma Purana* says that the center of the "U" should never be filled in, for this spot is the abode of Vishnu (the lines on either side representing Brahma and Shiva). Because the center of the *tilak* is Vishnu's abode, some *sampradayas* place there a small *bindu* (a red dot) as a representation of Shri, the Goddess.

Although the forehead marking is the most conspicuous, Vaishnavas mark their bodies at thirteen central energy centers, reciting various names of the Lord while applying the *tilak* to each spot. This meditation is designed to promote the awareness that the body is a temple of Vishnu and is intended to be used in that way.

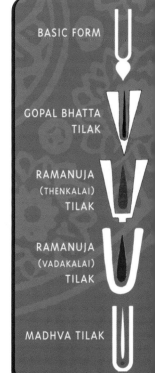

BASIC FORM

GOPAL BHATTA TILAK

RAMANUJA (THENKALAI) TILAK

RAMANUJA (VADAKALAI) TILAK

MADHVA TILAK

TILAK MANTRAS

The names of God that are chanted as one applies tilak markings, and the part of the body to which they are applied.

1 *Om keshavaya namah*
2 *Om narayanaya namah*
3 *Om madhavaya namah*
4 *Om govindaya namah*
5 *Om vishnave namah*
6 *Om madhusudanaya namah*
7 *Om trivikramaya namah*

8 *Om vamanaya namah*
9 *Om shridharaya namah*
10 *Om hrishikeshaya namah*
11 *Om padmanabhaya namah*
12 *Om damodaraya namah*
13 *Om vasudevaya namah*

SACRED
COW

Of all creatures, the COW is given a special place in the Indian religious tradition: "I speak to those who are aware: do not harm the cow, for, in so doing, you are harming the earth and all of humanity."

— *Rig Veda* 8.101.15

Despite the veneration bestowed upon the cow, there is no formal worship of a "cow-goddess" in Hindu temples. Rather, the cow is respected in her own right as one of humankind's seven mothers because she offers her milk as does one's natural mother. Gandhi himself had the highest regard for cows: "To me,

the cow is the embodiment of the whole infra-human world; she enables the believer to grasp his unity with all that lives....To protect her is to protect all the creatures of God's creation."

The five products of the cow (*pancha-gavya*)—milk, curd, ghee [clarified butter], urine, and dung—are all considered purifying. Cows

play a central role in India's economy. For example, cow dung serves as an inexpensive fertilizer. It is sometimes stored in underground tanks, where it generates methane gas that is used for heating and cooking. Cow dung is also a valuable disinfectant and is used both as a poultice and a cleansing agent.

Traditionally, the cow is considered dear to Lord Krishna. Indeed, Krishna is often known as "Gopal" and "Govinda"—names that refer to His loving feeling for cows. The very names of Krishna's holy land of Braj ("pasture") and His spiritual abode Goloka ("cow-world") reveal His intimate connection with bovine creatures. Krishna's love for the cow is celebrated throughout the Vedic literature. It is no wonder, therefore, that in the Vedas we find great emphasis on *ahimsa*, or harmlessness to all sentient beings, and especially on cow protection.

in the epic work *Mahabharata*: "The very name of the cows is *aghnya*, indicating that they should never be slaughtered. Who, then, could slay them? Surely, one who kills a cow or a bull commits the most heinous crime." (*Shanti-parva* 262.47)

The Vedic reference book *Nighantu* offers nine Sanskrit names for the cow, three of which—*aghnya* ("not to be killed"), *ahi* ("not be killed") and *aditi* ("not to be cut")—specifically forbid slaughter. The synonyms for "cow" are summarized

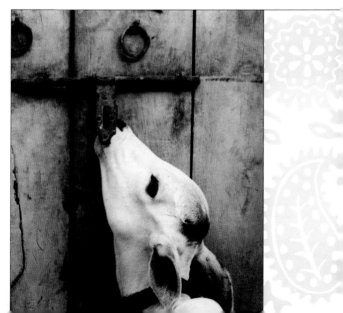

Vegetarianism

That vegetarianism has always been **widespread** in India is clear from even a cursory reading of India's traditional religious literature. The *Manu-smriti* (5.49), a Vedic guide for **human behavior**, says, "Having well considered the origin of flesh foods and the cruelty of fettering and slaying corporeal beings, let man entirely abstain from eating flesh." The same work (6.12) mentions that the eating of meat "involves killing, and consequently leads to karmic bondage [*bandha*]."

In the *Mahabharata* the great warrior Bhishma explains to Yudhishthir, eldest of the Pandava princes, that the meat of animals is like the flesh of one's own son; eating meat is repugnant. The *Mahabharata* emphasizes this point. The *brahmanas* of ancient India exalted cleanliness to a divine principle, but the eating of "dirty" food, the *Mahabharata* warns, is not as terrible as the eating of flesh.

The *Mahabharata* further explains, "Meat-eating is in the darker modes of existence, causing ignorance and disease." It explains that a healthy vegetarian diet is sattvic—that is, in the mode of goodness—able to increase purity of consciousness and longevity.

The Vedic scriptures do not limit their discussion of food to the avoidance of killing and the virtues of a vegetarian diet. According to Vedic texts, one should offer all food as a sacrifice to God: "All that you do, all that you eat, all that you offer and give away, as well as all austerities that you may perform," Lord Krishna says, "should be done as an offering unto Me." (*Bhagavad-gita* 9.27) One should not conclude, however, that everything is offerable. The *Gita* specifies exactly what should be offered: "If one offers Me with love and devotion a leaf, a flower, a fruit, or water, I will accept it." (9.26) Other references in the Vedic literature confirm that fruits, vegetables, grain, nuts, and dairy products are fit for human consumption. Followers of the *Gita* refrain from meat, fish, poultry, or

eggs, since these are not sanctioned by either the scriptures or the Vedic prophets.

The *Bhagavad-gita* further declares that one who lovingly offers his food to God according to scriptural guidelines is freed from all sinful reactions and consequent rebirth in the material world: "The devotees of the Lord are released from all kinds of sins because they eat food which is first offered in sacrifice. Others, who prepare food for personal sense enjoyment, verily eat only sin." (3.13) The remnants of such devotional offerings are called *prasadam* (literally "the Lord's mercy").

Most temples in India freely distribute sanctified vegetarian foods (*prasadam*) for the benefit of the multitudes who approach the holy shrines daily. One of the most celebrated Vedic sages, Narada Muni, was inspired to embark on the spiritual path merely by tasting food offered to the Lord.

Of the many contemporary movements based on Vedic philosophy and religion, the International Society for Krishna Consciousness (ISKCON) is noteworthy for its support of vegetarianism, and specifically for distribution of *prasadam*. In the many ISKCON temples and restaurants only *prasadam*, sanctified vegetarian food, is served to the guests.

INSIGHTS ON VEGETARIANISM

"It is my view that the vegetarian manner of living, by its purely physical effect on the human temperament, would most beneficially influence the lot of mankind."
— Albert Einstein

"As long as men massacre animals, they will kill each other. Indeed, he who sows the seeds of murder and pain cannot reap joy and love."
— Pythagoras

"When a man wants to murder a tiger, he calls it sport; when a tiger wants to murder him, he calls it ferocity."
— George Bernard Shaw

"A dead cow or sheep lying in a pasture is recognized as carrion. The same sort of carcass dressed and hung up in a butcher's stall passes as food!"
— J. H. Kellogg

"The eating of meat extinguishes the seed of great compassion."
— *Mahaparinirvana Sutra*
(a Buddhist scripture)

"And the flesh of slain beasts in his body will become his own tomb. For I tell you truly, he who kills, kills himself, and whoso eats the flesh of slain beasts, eats the body of death."
— *The Essene Gospel of Peace*

"Every act of irreverence for life, every act which neglects life, which is indifferent to and wastes life, is a step towards the love of death. This choice man must make at every minute. Never were the consequences of the wrong choice as total and as irreversible as they are today. Never was the warning of the Bible so urgent: 'I have put before you life and death, blessing and curse. Choose life, that you and your children may live.' (*Deuteronomy* 30:19)"
— Erich Fromm

"The greatness of a nation and its moral progress can be measured by the way in which its animals are treated."
— Mahatma Gandhi

feStivALs

India is often called a land where there are "thirteen religious festivals in twelve months." A Vaisnava festival, however enlivening to the senses it may be, with its singing, dancing, large feasts, colorful decorations, elaborate rituals, dramatic performances, perhaps even gaily dressed elephants, is most significantly a spiritual event.

The vastness of the Vaishnava tradition allows for almost daily festivities. The scale of such celebrations may range from a *mahotsava* ("large festival") to a simple gathering in the home. The Kumbha Mela, the largest holy gathering in the world, brings together millions of ascetics and pilgrims, while the ceremony of the first feeding of solid food to one's child (*annaprashana*) requires nothing more than the presence of the father and the mother.

Every festival offers many layers of meaning, edifying in numerous ways the people who take part. People perform and attend festivals to purify themselves, to obtain the blessings of sages, to receive

religious instruction, and to experience a joyful respite from everyday life. Festival dates are observed in accordance with the Vaishnava calendar, which is calculated by the phases of the moon rather than by the orbit of the sun. As such, by our Gregorian calendar the dates observed appear to change each year. Below is a short list of the more important festivals.

In the month of Magh (January–February) the Magh Mela, a sort of Vaishnava counterpart to the much larger Kumbha Mela, takes place.

Also in Magh, just before the onset of Phalguna (February–March), all of India also witnesses the massive Maha Shivaratri, one of the continent's largest festivals. Although Maha Shivaratri is not a Vaishnava holiday as such, many Vaishnavas honor Shiva as Krishna's greatest devotee, and so they come together at this time to praise him.

In Phalguna (February–March) two festivals mark the Indian calendar: Gaura Purnima (the

appearance anniversary of Shri Chaitanya Mahaprabhu) and Holi (a festival that celebrates the advent of spring). On Holi, people vigorously spray each other with colored dyes. The showering with various colors commemorates one of Krishna's many lilas with the *gopis*.

Chaitra (March–April) is the time of Ramachandra's appearance in this world; celebrations with dramatic readings and performances of Sita and Rama's *lila* abound.

As April turns to May, many Vaishnavas prepare for the appearance of Nrisimhadeva, the ferocious man-lion incarnation of the Lord. So in Vaishakha (April–May) the famous Nrisimha Chaturdashi is welcomed with stories and plays about the boy saint Prahlad and his relationship to Nrisimha.

Jyeshtha (May–June) brings Buddha Purnima, which celebrates simultaneously Buddha's birth, enlightenment, and entry into nirvana. Vaishnavas see Buddha as an incarnation of Vishnu, so they too take part in this festival.

Ashadha (June–July) is the time of the great Ratha-yatra festival at Puri, a celebratory procession that, through the efforts of the International Society for Krishna Consciousness (ISKCON), now takes place in cities all over the world.

As the hot summer continues, Shravana (July–August) brings forth Naga Panchami—a glorification of Balaram (Krishna's elder brother) in His form of Shesha, the huge serpent who supports Vishnu with his divine coils.

Bhadra (August–September) is when Krishna Janmashtami (the holy appearance of Shri Krishna) is celebrated. This month is also famous for Radhashtami, the divine birthday of Radha, Shri Krishna's consort. Another important festival during this month is Ganesh Chaturthi, the day of the elephant-headed god Ganesh.

In Ashvin (September–October) there is a special festival connected to Durga Puja, and a long stream of diverse celebrations ending with the defeat of Ravana, the villain of the Ramayana. Ashvin teaches us that goodness wins out in the end; as such, throughout the streets of India, gigantic effigies of the tyrant Ravana are set ablaze.

Kartik (October–November) is celebrated as a month-long Vaishnava mahotsava, during which Divali, the Festival of Lights, takes place. It is roughly at this time, too, that Govardhan Puja is celebrated—a festival that shows Krishna's supremacy over other gods.

This is but a small sampling of the endless festival that is Vaishnava *dharma*.

The modes of nature

The concept of the three modes of material nature is an integral part of the Vaishnava worldview. According to this concept, material existence is understood in terms of three essential characteristics: sattva (goodness, virtue), rajas (exertion, passion, turbulence), and tamas (inertia, ignorance).

The word "mode" is a loose translation of the Sanskrit word *guna*, which literally means "thread" or "rope" (implying that goodness, passion, and ignorance are the ropes that bind individuals to the material world). These constituent qualities underlie everything we see, hear, taste, touch, and smell. The entire world, in fact, is made up of various permutations of these qualities, and like the primary colors red, blue, and yellow, the *gunas* can be mixed in unlimited ways, producing uncountable variations.

Sattva is associated with virtues and qualities such as wisdom, joy, and altruism; *rajas* with ambition, greed, frustration, and anger; and *tamas* with idleness, sloth, and delusion. In the Varnashrama system, for example, *brahmanas* are considered to be in the mode of goodness, *kshatriyas* in the mode of passion, *vaishyas* in passion and ignorance combined, and *shudras* in ignorance.

The three modes are often described as clarifying, confusing, and obscuring, or as pacifying, impelling, and impeding, respectively.

In the Vaishnava tradition each mode is associated with a principal deity: Vishnu, the Supreme Godhead, who maintains the cosmic manifestation, is master of the mode of goodness; Brahma, the creator demigod, predominates over passion; and Shiva, the destroyer, presides over ignorance.

In a given person's life, a particular mode predominates, and this conditions the way he or she behaves. Understanding how one is conditioned by the modes, and how the modes are interacting with the consciousness, helps an individual achieve stability and happiness. Still, one should aspire to become detached from all three modes, even from goodness. Although goodness embodies finer material qualities, such qualities are still material and can serve as "the last infirmity of a noble mind," as indologist A.L. Basham has said, "causing the soul to cling to wisdom and joy as opposed to God consciousness proper."

The first systematic analysis of the modes occurs in the *Bhagavad-gita*, which devotes to this subject 100 of its 700 verses. According to the *Gita*,

God, as the creator of the modes, is naturally above them, but the ordinary soul is not. The *Gita's* fourteenth chapter outlines the general characteristics of the modes and tells of the importance of understanding and thus rising beyond them. The seventeenth chapter analyzes the workings of the modes in the areas of worship, sacrifices, and austerities, in the food one eats, and even in the way one distributes gifts. Essentially, the *Gita* brings into focus the subtleties of the three modes and helps us understand distinct personality types resulting from these modes.

THE THREE MODES IN OTHER TRADITIONS

Other traditions have elaborated upon tripartite categories that correspond to personality types. Plato, for example, discusses the rational soul, the spirited soul, and the appetitive soul. This refers to the intellectual, contemplative person, the pugnacious and overly active person, and the self-centered braggart, respectively. Plato acknowledges that all three personality types can be found in any given individual, but inevitably, as with the three modes of nature, one personality type will predominate.

Certain schools of modern psychology acknowledge three somatotypes, or body types: ectomorphy (thin), mesomorphy (muscular), and endomorphy (fat). It is said that these correspond to certain mental dispositions: cerebrotonia (brain-oriented), somatotonia (muscle-oriented), and viscerotonia (stomach-heart–oriented). Scholars of Indian religion, such as A. L. Herman, professor of philosophy at the University of Wisconsin–Stevens Point, have noted that, while this taxonomy does not directly correspond to the three modes of material nature, there is enough similarity to warrant further research. Nonetheless, as Herman acknowledges, the *Gita* provides one of the most penetrating psychological analyses of individuals and their conditional responses to the material world.

Ayurveda

Ayurveda ("the science of life") is an ancient system of natural healing. Predating the Chinese system of medicine, the fundamentals of Ayurvedic science were put into written form (in the Atharva Veda) some fifty centuries ago. The Ayurvedic science gives highly detailed explanations of sophisticated medical techniques and is said to have been brought to this world by an incarnation of Vishnu known as Dhanvantari.

Twenty-five hundred years ago, the science was systematized by the sages Charaka and Sushruta, acknowledged as the founding fathers of health and healing. Sushruta, who is the originator of Ayurvedic surgery, conducted complicated and delicate surgical procedures, such as caesareans, cataract operations, and brain surgery.

Charaka and Sushruta's works—the *Charaka-samhita* and the *Sushruta-samhita*—are still extant. These detailed medical books are greatly revered because the ancient Vedic doctors who wrote them were mystics, seers (*rishis*), and were able to apprehend the inner workings of the human body through insights gained in meditation. Today one can confirm these insights by comparing ancient Vedic medicine to modern medical discoveries (the Vedic texts, for example, describe in detail the month-by-month development of the fetus).

Ayurveda contains a vast body of knowledge, with subjects ranging

from pediatrics, obstetrics, internal medicine, gynecology, and otolaryngology to anesthesiology, artificial limb construction, and plastic surgery.

Ayurveda explains the human psychophysical condition in terms of three *doshas* ("humors"): *vata* (air, or wind), *pitta* (fire, or bile), and *kapha* (earth, or phlegm). Based on a person's overall constitution, one of these three humors will predominate. Illness, say Ayurvedic texts, is due to an imbalance in the three vital humors.

According to *Ayurveda*, health can be restored through a proper balancing of the *doshas*. *Doshas* are

Ayurvedic treatment involves natural herbs and holistic medicine.

balanced through highly individual corrections in diet, regulated daily activity, and good hygiene, environment, and thought patterns. The medicinal use of food and herbs is a prominent part of Ayurvedic science and is determined for each individual according to body type, or constitution.

Unfortunately, due to foreign conquests as well as internal conflicts in India, in due course of time *Ayurveda* became obscure. It is once again gaining in recognition, however, both by holistic and by allopathic schools of thought. There are currently hundreds of universities in India devoted to its study, and in America there is a school of surgeons called the Sushruta Society. *Ayurveda* has become of interest around the world.

Above: Vishnu, in His form as Mohini-murti, distributes nectar which frees one from invalidity, old age, and death.
Right: Dhanvantari, the incarnation of Vishnu who founded Ayurveda.

VEDIC ASTROLOGY

Astrology has been a recognized science in India from the earliest times. The Vedic wisdom, in addition to its main body of literature, includes six angas, or ancillary sections. One of them is Jyotish—astronomy and astrology.

Jyotish (literally "light") describes the planets, stars, and other heavenly bodies. Early Indian astronomers divided the sky into twelve parts called *rashis* (constellations). Each *rashi* was given a name according to a form it resembled. For example, the first sign, which is in the shape of a ram, was called Mesha (ram). In Western terminology, Mesha is called Aries. Some other examples: Taurus = Rishabha (bull), Leo = Simha (lion). When a particular sign is seen on the horizon from a specific region of the earth, a person born there at that time is said to be born in that sign.

Vedic astrology has five basic subdivisions: *jataka* (natal), *prashna* (divining), *varshaphala* (predictive), *muhurta* (electional), and *yatra* (mundane). Each subdivision has its own methods of calculation for interpreting data.

The methods of Vedic astrology differ from those of its Western counterpart, although there is some overlapping and interrelation between the two. The areas of excellence of each school differ as well. Western astrology, some say, more clearly defines personality types and characteristics, while Vedic astrology more accurately predicts events and circumstances.

It is said that a qualified Vedic astrologer can determine specific facts about an individual's karma (previous activities) and, consequently, his or her destiny. Two points are significant in this context. First, few qualified Vedic astrologers exist today (the science requires years of study, and intuitive wisdom). Secondly, Vaishnavas generally use astrological data as an adjunct to knowledge received from the Vedas. Astrology is considered merely an aid, not an ultimate source of knowledge. For Vaishnavas, Krishna is in control. He honors the living being's free will, and thus destiny can be changed.

ASTROLOGICAL APPLICATION

An important aspect of astrology is known as *muhurta,* or "the proper time at which to begin an endeavor." For example, there are auspicious and inauspicious times to begin a business enterprise or perform a marriage. Currently at Benares Hindu University there is a Jyotish department, whose offices produce the annual astrological calendar; this serves the entire Hindu world by determining the exact dates for sacred days and appropriate times for public functions.

Vedic deities preside over the various planets: Budh (Mercury), Sukra (Venus), Chandra (Moon), Mangal (Mars), Surya (Sun), Guru (Jupiter), Sanee (Saturn), Kethu (South Node), and Rahu (North Node).

THE GAYATRI MANTRA ॐ

The **sacred** Gayatri mantra has been chanted on the banks of holy rivers in India for millennia. One can visualize an Indian holy man, sitting with legs folded in the traditional lotus posture, looking out into the countless waves of the Ganges, as *brahmanas* have for countless generations. He wraps around his finger the sacred thread (*upavita*), on which the mantra is chanted, and murmers sacred sounds that only he and the Lord can hear. It is the Brahma-gayatri mantra, known to all *brahmanas* and Vaishnavas.

The Gayatri mantra is confidential; it is whispered by the teacher in the disciple's right ear, for scriptures say that unless received in this fashion the mantra is useless. We will not, therefore, reproduce it here. The mantra pays homage to the sun and is chanted three times a day: as the sun rises, when it is high in the sky, and when it sets. In the Vaishnava tradition the sun represents God because, like God, it illuminates all that is.

Gaudiya Vaishnavas chant several Gayatri mantras. In addition to the Brahma-gayatri, they chant two prayers to the guru, two to Chaitanya Mahaprabhu, and two to Krishna. Although Vaishnavas consider all seven of these mantras to be Gayatris, in a technical sense they are not. To be an actual Gayatri, a mantra should include the words *vidmahe* (the approach), *dhimahi* (the path), and *prachodayat* (the goal). Interestingly, this aligns the Gayatri mantra with the *Shrimad Bhagavatam* (the most important of all Vaishnava scriptures), whose three underlying themes are *sambandha* (*vidmahe*), *abhidheya* (*dhimahi*), and *prayojana* (*prachodayat*).

Thus, the Gayatri mantra and the *Shrimad Bhagavatam* are one in meaning and purpose—both lead to the path of liberation.

Four of the seven "Gayatri" mantras chanted by Vaishnavas are actually Gayatris in the strictest sense. The other three mantras are nonetheless equally important, for one of them is an introductory prayer to the guru, another is a similar introductory prayer to Mahaprabhu, and the third is the Gopal-mantra, considered one of the most important mantras of the Gaudiya-Vaishnava Sampradaya, as it establishes the supremacy of the *gopis* and their unequalled love for Krishna. Deep meditation on all of these mantras brings the practitioner to a state of clear consciousness and pure goodness. This allows for a more profound practice of the *maha-mantra*—Hare Krishna, Hare Krishna, Krishna Krishna, Hare Hare/Hare Rama, Hare Rama, Rama Rama, Hare Hare.

> "I am the syllable *om* in the Vedic mantras."
> —Lord Krishna, *Bhagavad-gita 7.8*

According to the Upanishads, *om* is the sound representation of the Supreme; it is the impersonal Brahman in vibratory form. Although most refer to om (or *a-u-m*) as having no distinct translation, the word consists of the first (a) and last (u) vowel and the last consonant (m) of the Sanskrit alphabet; it is thus considered to be "the perfect word," encompassing "all truths that words can convey." In addition, *a* is said to represent waking consciousness, *u*, dream consciousness, and *m*, deep sleep. Thus *a-u-m* represents the totality of consciousness.

In India's spiritual tradition, *a-u-m* is seen as the *pranava* (*omkara*), or the mystic syllable, and thus has a distinct Vaishnava meaning: the letter *a* (*a-kara*) refers to Krishna, the beginningless beginning and the source of all energy; the letter *u* (*u-kara*) indicates Radharani, the Lord's spiritual pleasure potency, the embodiment of all divine energies; and *m* (*ma-kara*) refers to all living entities (*jivas*), who are meant to use their energy in the service of the Lord. Thus to Vaishnavas, *om* represents the sum and substance of spiritual energy and the totality of existence.

By reciting the Gayatri mantra, shown on the left in her personified form as Gayatri-devi, Lord Brahma was able to create the multifarious universes.

Sound

Portions of the Vedic literature are almost like textbooks on sound, elucidating the use of sound as a **spiritual tool**. The same concept is echoed in other cultures. Chronicles from lands as diverse as Egypt and Ireland tell us of a time when vibrations lying at the foundation of our universe were harnessed by spiritual adepts for the benefit of mankind. Like the Bible, which states, "**In the beginning was the Word**" (John 1:1), Vaishnava scriptures affirm that the entire cosmic creation began with sound: "By His utterance came the universe." (*Brihad-aranyaka Upanishad* 1.2.4) The *Vedanta-sutras* add that ultimate liberation comes from sound as well (*anavrittih shabdat*).

Primal sound is referred to as Shabda Brahman—God as word. Closely related to this is the concept of Nada Brahman—God as sound. *Nada*, a Sanskrit word meaning "sound," is related to the term *nadi*, denoting the stream of consciousness—a concept that goes back to the *Rig Veda*, the most ancient of the Vedas. Thus, the relationship between sound and consciousness has long been recorded in India's ancient literature. Vedic texts, in fact, describe sound as the preeminent means for attaining higher, spiritual consciousness.

Mantras, or sacred sounds, are used to pierce through sensual, mental and intellectual levels of existence—all lower strata of consciousness—for the purpose of purification and spiritual enlightenment. The sounds of different letters, particularly Sanskrit letters, have been shown to affect the mind, intellect, and auditory nerves of those who chant and hear them. The seven energy centers (*chakras*) of the spinal column, as well as the *ida*, *pingala*, and *sushumna nadis*, or the three pranic channels of the subtle body, all respond to mantras, bringing practitioners to elevated levels of awareness.

THE UNHEARD WORLD OF SOUND

Engulfed by every imaginable type of sound, man in the current age no longer truly hears. In fact, human beings are physically unable to perceive certain portions of the known vibratory spectrum. While being extremely sensitive to sound waves of about 1,000 to 4,000 cycles per second (cps), man is all but deaf beyond 20,000 cycles per second. Dogs and cats, on the other hand, can hear up to 60,000 cps, while mice, bats, whales, and dolphins can emit and receive sounds well over 100,000 cps.

Despite our inability to hear certain frequencies, comparatively speaking we still hear better than we see. This idea is further explained by Katharine Le Mee in her book *Chant* (New York: Bell Tower Publishing, 1994, pp. 28–29):

"The sense of hearing ... connects experientially with the heart, and music and sound touch us most directly. We do not resonate so deeply with the visual as with the auditory. This may be explained by the fact that our visual apparatus has a frequency range of slightly less than one octave, from infrared to ultraviolet, whereas our auditory system has a range of about eight octaves, approximately 60 to 16,000 hertz, or number of vibrations per second. We are sensitive to sound frequency as pitch and to light frequency as color. The frequencies of the visual field are much higher than those of the auditory field (by an order of 1010), and, as is well known, the higher the frequencies, the lesser the penetration of a given material. For instance, a piece of cardboard shields us easily from the light, but it takes a thick wall to block out sound, and the lower the pitch the deeper the penetration. We are very sensitive to sound, not just through the ear but through our whole skin, and all our organs are affected by it."

Science has shown that human senses are imperfect and limited, and that there is a world of sensual experience beyond human perception. Vaishnava scriptures confirm these limitations in man's seeing and hearing and elucidate untold categories of spiritual sound.

CHANTING

(Krishna says:)
"I dwell not in the spiritual kingdom,
nor in the hearts of yogis;
where My devotees are chanting,
there, O Narada, stand I!" — *Padma Purana*

Vaishnava texts state that in much the same way that one could awaken a person who is sleeping by making a sound or calling out his name, man can awaken himself from his conditioned, materialistic slumber by calling out the name of God. In fact, the world's major religious traditions concur that it is by chanting the name of God that one attains enlightenment and freedom from materialistic conditioning.

Mohammed counseled, "Glorify the name of your Lord, the most high." (Koran 87.2); Saint Paul said, "Everyone who calls upon the name of the Lord will be saved." (*Romans* 10.13); Buddha declared, "All who sincerely call upon my name will come to me after death, and I will take them to paradise." (*Vows of Amida Buddha* 18); King David preached, "From the rising of the sun to its setting, the name of the Lord is to be praised." (*Psalms* 113.3); and

the Vaishnava scriptures repeatedly assert: "Chant the holy name, chant the holy name, chant the holy name of the Lord. In this Age of Quarrel there is no other way, no other way, no other way to attain spiritual enlightenment." (*Brihan-naradiya Purana* 3.8.126)

Praise of the holy name of God is found throughout the literature of the Vaishnavas: "Oh, how glorious are they whose tongues are chanting Your holy name! Even if originally low-born dog-eaters, they are to be considered worshipable. To have reached the point of chanting the Lord's name, they must have executed various austerities and Vedic sacrifices and achieved all the good qualities of true Aryans. If they are chanting Your holy name, they must have bathed in all holy rivers, studied the Vedas and fulfilled all prescribed duties." (*Shrimad Bhagavatam* 3.33.7)

"The holy name of Krishna is the spiritually blissful giver of

all benedictions, for it is Krishna Himself, the reservoir of pleasure. Krishna's name is complete in itself and is the essential form of all spiritual relationships. It is not a material name under any condition, and it is no less powerful than Krishna Himself. This name is not tinged by any aspect of material nature, because it is identical with Krishna." (*Padma Purana* 3.21)

Because chanting the name of God is so much emphasized in Vaishnava texts, practitioners focus on chanting as a central devotional method. Thus, deep meditation and great emotion accompany *japa* (the soft chanting), *kirtan* (the loud chanting), and *sankirtan* (the congregational chanting). When perfected, the chanting leads to awareness of God's absolute nature, i.e., that there is no difference between the *nami* ("the named one") and *nama* ("the name"). Absorption in the absolute nature of Krishna and His name is the heart of Vaishnava mysticism, leading to love of God.

Norvin Hein, Professor Emeritus at Yale University, has witnessed enthusiastic Gaudiya-Vaishnava *kirtan*, and in writing about it he captures its most emotional components:

"In the singing of verses like these, each line, separately, is incanted by the leader first, and the whole assembly repeats each line after him, one by one. As the verse is gone through again and again, the leader steps up the tempo. When the speed of utterance approaches the utmost possible, the whole group, in unison, begins to shout the lines, at the same time beating out the rhythm with sharply-timed clapping of hands. The singers begin to sway and let themselves go in ungoverned gestures. Faces flush. From the line of instrumental accompanists the bell-like peal of small brass cymbals swells up with the rising shouting and pierces through it. The whole process approaches a crashing, breathtaking crescendo. The point of explosion is reached: eyes flash, mouths drop open, a tremor runs through the entire assembly. The Power, the Presence, has been felt!"[1]

Notes

1. Norvin Hein, 1976. "Caitanya's Ecstasies and the Theology of the Name," in Hinduism: New Essays in the History of Religions, 22–23. Leiden: E. J. Brill.

THE MAHA MANTRA

The Hare Krishna *maha-mantra*, or "the great chant for deliverance," is considered by scripture the most powerful of mantras, for it includes the potency of all others.

The mantra runs as follows: Hare Krishna, Hare Krishna, Krishna Krishna, Hare Hare/Hare Rama, Hare Rama, Rama Rama, Hare Hare, and the Vedic literature particularly recommends it for the current age. Statements to this effect can be found in the *Brahmanda Purana*, the *Kalisantarana Upanishad*, and in many other Vedic and post-Vedic texts.

Breaking down the sacred mantra into its component parts: The word "Hare" refers to Lord Hari—a name for Krishna that indicates His ability to remove obstacles from His devotees' path. In a higher sense, the word "Hare" is a vocative form of "Hara," which refers to Mother Hara, or Shrimati Radharani, the divine feminine energy.

"Krishna" means "the all-attractive one," referring to God in His original form. Etymologically, the word *krish* indicates the attractive feature of the Lord's existence, and *na* means spiritual pleasure. When the verb *krish* is combined with the affix *na*, we have *krishna*, which means "the absolute person, who gives spiritual pleasure through His all-attractive qualities." According to Sanskrit semantic derivation (*nirukti*), it is also understood that *na* refers to the Lord's ability to stop the repetition of birth and death. And *krish* is a synonym for *sattartha*, or "existential totality." Another way of understanding the word *krishna*, then, is "that Lord who embodies all of existence and who can help the living entities overcome the repeated suffering of birth and death."

"Rama" refers to both Balaram (Krishna's elder brother) and also Radha-Ramana-Rama, which is a name for Krishna meaning "one who brings pleasure to Shrimati

Radharani." Thus the *maha-mantra*, composed solely of the Lord's most confidential names, embodies the essence of the Divine. As a prayer, the mantra is translated in the following way: "O Lord, O divine energy of the Lord! Please engage me in Your service."

Above: Radha and Krishna, the ultimate divine couple evoked by the maha-mantra.
Left: Krishna and His elder brother, Balaram.
Top: Shri Chaitanya chants the maha-mantra and dances with His associates.

Hare Krishna, Hare Krishna, Krishna Krishna, Hare Hare
Hare Rama, Hare Rama, Rama Rama, Hare Hare

Afterword
Vaishnavism comes West

Five hundred years ago, Shri Chaitanya predicted that in every town and village of the world the names of Krishna would be sung. This prediction was reiterated in the early twentieth century by Shrila Bhaktivinode Thakur, who prophesied that a time was soon coming when "Russians, Europeans, Americans, and all others will raise banners in glorification of Krishna and will together sing the names of Hari." History tells of a few attempts to introduce Vaishnavism to the West, most notably by Bhaktivinode himself, who wrote extensively in English and sent several of his works to Western shores.

Around the time of Bhaktivinode's endeavor, "the American Transcendentalists," as they were called, luminaries such as Emerson and Thoreau, were discovering Sanskrit, the language of the Vedas, and scholars were translating the previously unreadable texts of India into languages of the West. A deep appreciation of Eastern culture thus began to sweep all lands west of the Ganges, preparing the ground for the blossoming of a devotional renaissance.

Archaeological evidence shows that much earlier—in the second century B.C.E.—Heliodorus, a Greek ambassador to India, erected in Central India a pillar, on which he declared himself "a Bhagavat," i.e., a devotee of Bhagavan. In other words, he was an adherent of the Vaishnava religion. Thomas Hopkins, Professor of Religion at Franklin and Marshall College, suggests that if Heliodorus was a Western devotee of Krishna, there must have been many others. Thus, the interaction of Vaishnavism and the West has a long, noteworthy history.

It was not until the modern era, however, that the real heart of Eastern culture was brought to the West. This started slowly. Perhaps as a result of the early "Transcendentalists" (and their "Beat Poet" disciples), Buddhism and Hinduism became curiosities throughout the Occident by the turn of the twentieth century. But to this day, the versions of these religions that circulate in the West have largely been adulterated by notions from what has come to be called the "New Age." Respected writers, such as Donald Lopez and Huston Smith, bemoan the fact that Western brands

From left to right: Shrila Bhaktivinode Thakura, Shrila Bhaktisiddhanta Sarasvati Thakur, and His Divine Grace A. C. Bhaktivedanta Swami Prabhupada.

of Buddhism and Hinduism have set aside many of the traditional values and practices in favor of accommodationist techniques and compromised spiritual regimens. Consequently, experts say, Buddhism and Hinduism in the West have now both become virtually different religions. To a large extent, for orthodox practitioners in the East the Hindu yoga and the Buddhist chanting now popular in the West are hardly recognizable.

And though the scholarly study of Vaishnavism is now more prevalent than ever before, with courses in the *Bhagavad-gita* and Vaishnava spirituality in many Ivy League universities, few of the students taking these courses ever become devotees of Krishna—nearly all remain outsiders looking in. True, members of various Vaishnava lineages have sporadically come West, but few of these adventurous sadhus made a lasting impression, nor were they able to transplant the tradition fully, roots and all. Even Shrila Bhaktisiddhanta Sarasvati Thakur, the guru of His Divine Grace A. C. Bhaktivedanta Swami Prabhupada, sent several of his disciples to America and Europe in the 1930s—but he too found that his followers were not up to the task

and that the ground was not yet fertile.

All of this was to change when Vaishnavism's most powerful presence in the West was established in 1965 by His Divine Grace A. C. Bhaktivedanta Swami Prabhupada. Shrila Prabhupada was able to accomplish what none of the others were able to: He brought Vaishnava culture, in its entirety, into the hearts of Westerners, and gave new momentum to the movement in the East as well. He did this by himself embodying pure devotion and incomparable scholarship. But more, his compassion allowed him to reach out to men, women, and children throughout the world. His mission continues to thrive, with temples, farms, schools, restaurants, and publishing houses worldwide.

The work of Heliodorus and others like him is only a dim memory; the poetry of the Transcendentalists and their disciples gave only an expurgated derivative of true Vedic culture; and the early missionary activity of prior Vaishnavas had little effect. Shrila Prabhupada, on the other hand, was able to do the undoable. It was he who took the prediction of Shri Chaitanya and made it a tangible reality that is here to stay.

CREDITS

Project coordination: Brahma Muhurta Das
Prepress management: Kanjalochana Das
Design and layout: Ian Szymkowiak (Palace Press International)
Assistant designers: Chris Bryant, Alan Hebel (Palace Press International)
Initial design and picture research: Barbara Berasi-Rosen
Prepress and additional layout: Govinda Cordua
Assistant picture researchers: Nagaraj Das, Tridham Das, Yamaraj Das
Content editors: Gopiparanadhana Das, Dravida Das, Barbara Berasi-Rosen
Copy editor: Stuart Hensley Oates
Assistant copy editor: Gabriela Oates
Proofreader: Ksama Dasi
Cartographic design: Barbara Berasi-Rosen

The Bhaktivedanta Book Trust photographers: Bhargava Das, Govinda Das, Murlivadana Das, Nitya-tripta Dasi, Vishakha Dasi, Yadubar Das, Yamaraj Das.

The Bhaktivedanta Book Trust artists: Baradraj Das, Charuhasa Das, Devahuti Dasi, Dhriti Dasi, Dinabandhu Das, Dirgha Dasi, Jadurani Dasi, Jagat Karana Dasi, Janmanalaya Das, Jaya Rama Das, Murlidhar Das, Pandu Das, Pariksit Das, Pushkar Das, Ramanath Das, Ramdas Abhiram Das, Ranchor Das, Sulakshman Dasi, Vajra Lakshmi Dasi.

Thanks to the BBTI Review Board.

The publisher thanks the following photographers, painters, and organizations for their kind permission to reproduce their images in this book:

(Abbreviations: **B** bottom; **C** center; **T** top; **L** left; **R** right)

Angelo F. Dinoto (Amritamsa Das) (www.starprojectdesign.com/dinotosite/dinoto.html), photographs on front cover and on pages: 3, 4T, 5BL, 8B, 8L, 9BR, 10L, 11T, 11BL, 32L, 33TR, 104, 120L, 130, 131, 134L, 134TR, 146T, 146C, 153, 169, 174, 175, 184TR (© Mandala Publishing)

Indra Sharma, art on pages: 20C, 25TR, 36L, 37, 50B, 54, 55C, 55BR, 64L, 76L, 77, 126B, 147B (© Mandala Publishing)

B. G. Sharma, art on pages: 26L, 27B, 28B, 79T (© Mandala Publishing)

Mandala Archive, photographs on pages: 113B, 115BL, 168L (© Mandala Publishing)

Helmut Kappel, photographs on pages: 67BR, 170TC, 171BR

Every effort has been made to trace copyright holders. However, if there are any ommissions we would be happy to correct them in future editions.

THE AUTHOR

Steven J. Rosen was initiated into the esoteric tradition of Gaudiya Vaishnavism in 1975 by the esteemed Vaishnava teacher His Divine Grace A. C. Bhaktivedanta Swami Prabhupada. Prabhupada gave Rosen the name Satyaraja Das, which means "Servant of the King of Truth". In pursuance of that Truth, Rosen has written twenty books on East Indian spirituality and for the past decade has served as the senior editor of *The Journal of Vaishnava Studies*. His latest books include *Gita on the Green: The Mystical Tradition Behind Bagger Vance* (New York: Continuum International, 2002); *Holy War: Violence and the Bhagavad Gita* (Virginia: Deepak Heritage Books, 2002); and *From Nothingness to Personhood: A Collection of Essays on Buddhism from a Vaishnava-Hindu Perspective* (New York: FOLK Books, 2003).